Radical Islam vs. America

Benjamin Hart

Green Hill Publishers, Inc.
Ottawa, Illinois

Copyright © 2003 by Traditional Values Coalition

Mail Orders and bulk copy purchase: 1-800-426-1357

T.V.C.
P.O. Box 738
Ottawa, IL 61350

Printed in the United States of America
ISBN 0-915463-90-3

7 6 5 4 3 2 1 / 05 04 03

Contents

Foreword

Most Americans have friends who are followers of mainstream Islam. They live in communities all over the country and are among our most peaceful and productive citizens. Any suggestion that these Muslims, who believe in a kind and loving God, are a threat to other Americans must be rejected as either ignorant or ill-willed. Ben Hart's book—as he makes clear at the outset—is not about them.

However, in seeking to spare our Muslim friends from prejudice and persecution, we must not oversimplify the current crisis by saying, as did British Prime Minister Tony Blair, that the attack on the World Trade Center "had nothing to do with Islam."

In truth, it had everything to do with Islam, though not with the religion of "Submission" practiced by a majority of Muslims worldwide.

The Ayatollah Khomeini, Usama bin Laden, and the suicide bombers of Jerusalem and New York believe in a different Prophet, a different Allah, and a different ethic from those professed by the moderate majority. Like Satan when tempting Christ, these militant Muslims can quote scripture—chapter and verse from the Koran—to justify suicide, murder, and the mass starvation of the poor victims they call "infidels."

Muslim zealots are killing Jews in the Middle East and Christians in Sudan and Indonesia.

They are developing nuclear, chemical, and biological weapons designed to annihilate great masses of humanity.

And all of these atrocities, they believe, are committed according to the will of Allah.

In nations dominated by this wild strain of Islamic thought, Christians and Jews are not allowed to build houses of worship, attend public worship, or exchange religious literature. In such countries, Islamic law decrees that a Muslim who converts to Christianity or Judaism must be put to death.

Americans are not used to enemies who take religion so seriously. We tend to think of modern warfare in terms of territorial disputes, trade barriers, and economic interests. These Muslims believe they are fighting for Allah and the Prophet— hence their willingness to die in order to kill unbelievers.

For the sake of our faith and future, we must understand precisely what these fanatics think and feel. Ben Hart's book is the only study of Islam available that forces us to look unblinkingly into the minds, hearts, and souls of militant Muslims by revealing in their own words just why they hate us—and what they intend to do to us.

These are some of the most appalling statements I have ever encountered. No one can read them without being profoundly shocked at the hatred and cruelty they reveal.

In order to help you understand the true nature of the enemy we face, I'm sending you, free, this vital book. I hope you'll read it, support our massive distribution by mail with a contribution, and also order copies to pass copies along to your friends. And please act quickly. I'm worried that our people won't understand the danger until it's too late.

—Rev. Louis P. Sheldon

Introduction

Neither the press nor the U.S. State Department has made a real effort to inform the public about the dangers we face in the so-called War Against Terror. Sure, we now have security screenings at airports and a new federal bureaucracy, but Western governments and the media keep telling us that—as Tony Blair put it—September 11 "has nothing to do with Islam."[1]

Moderate Islam does promote peace and tolerance. If a Muslim family lives next door, you needn't stock your closets with guns and ammunition and barricade the house every night. These people are no more likely to terrorize the neighborhood than the Christians on the corner or the Jews across the street.

On the other hand, militant Islam has its own unique religious tradition, a heritage that is more conducive to violence than that of contemporary Christianity or Judaism. The State Department's view, echoed by the President, that "Islam is peace"[2] isn't shared by every U.S. official who has studied Islamic history and culture. Larry Johnson, a former official at both the CIA and the Department of State, accuses our government of misrepresenting Islam to conform to a "bit of political correctness...."

"We like to portray as a nation, Islam is a religion of peace, and it really isn't," he said.

As it is widely practiced, [Islam] doesn't encourage peace and it encourages violence. Part of that is that it has not had its own version of the Reformation. It is stuck in the Middle Ages as Christianity or Judaism once was ...[Moderates] do not represent the majority thought in the Muslim world. They are very much on the defensive.

Yet those who argue that Islam promotes peace and tolerance have convinced a majority of the American people. Believe it or not, the approval rating of Muslim Americans jumped ten points after 9-11. However, our government and media have yet to convince the militant Middle Eastern sheikhs or their armed-and-dangerous followers that theirs is a peaceful religion. Throughout the region, militants are praising bin Laden, the attack on the World Trade Center, and the suicide bombers; justifying the killing of Christians and Jews with citations from the Qur'an; and calling for all Muslims to join in a holy war ("Jihad") to drive the infidels out of the Arabian peninsula. (If you don't know who the "infidels" are, read on.)

American politicians and the press continue to speak about the struggle in purely political and economic terms. But, in the Middle East, Indonesia, and Islamic Africa, the talk is about the Prophet and the Qur'an. This is not the typical modern conflict— a clash between nations over disputed territory or conflicting economic interests. The goals of Al Quaida transcend nationality and world trade. Its adherents are as militantly religious today as their predecessors in the seventh century. Short-term, their aim is to drive Christians and Jews from the Middle East. Long-term, it is the subjugation of the entire world to the will of Allah.

Again, a majority of American Muslims don't share this goal, or even think about it. There are an estimated one billion Muslims in the world today, only 15 percent of whom are Arab; and many Arabs reject the course of the Ayatollah Khomeini and Usama bin Laden. But the rest of them are the driving engine of the attack on Israel and the United States. There is strong support for bin

Laden and Al Quaida in Iraq, Iran, Syria, Pakistan, Afghanistan, and Saudi Arabia. Egyptian, Indonesian, and Sudanese Muslims have also lent their voices to the cause of holy war.

We have been told by American Muslim leaders and apologists that the word "Jihad" does not mean "holy war" but denotes instead "an inner striving" or "spiritual struggle." Yet in numerous statements by Arab and African religious leaders, "Jihad" is specifically used to mean a war fought in the name of Allah and his Prophet. To put it bluntly, Jihad means killing Christians and Jews.

A failure to see the dark side of Islam has already caused us to underestimate the fierce resolve of our enemies, thereby failing to take them seriously enough. These are people who are willing to blow themselves to smithereens in a crowded bus in order to kill ten noncombatant Jews.

This kind of ultimate commitment is not merely the product of patriotism. It grows out of a deep and abiding faith in Allah, who rewards his martyrs with eternal joy and punishes the rest of us with the fires of hell. If we want to know why those September hijackers deliberately rammed planes into steel and concrete buildings, we must look at the religious beliefs they held, the hopes they entertained, the God they thought they served.

What follows, then, is not a discussion of Islam in all its complexity. The moderate Muslims have their historians and defenders, people who can testify that they are in no way to blame for the current wave of terrorism sweeping the world. Most Muslims want freedom, prosperity, and democracy, like everyone else. *This book is not about them.*

This book focuses instead on *militant* Islam—on the suicide bombers and the clergy who urge them to sacrifice their lives, on the killers of women and children, and on the theology that justifies such outrageous acts. We must remember that these Muslims are not the equivalent of street gangs, cultists, or the lone - assassins of American presidents. They belong to a religious community that numbers in the millions. Several key Middle Eastern, African, and Eastern nations are controlled by such factions.

This book is about them.

Specifically, it deals with three misconceptions popularized by our political leadership and the mass media.

First, it takes up the idea that Islam is a religion of peace and that "Jihad" means "inner struggle" or "spiritual discipline"— anything but "holy war." The differing interpretations of this concept are the result of seemingly contradictory attitudes expressed by the Prophet in the Qur'an. However, we need be concerned with only one definition of this word—the one that resulted in the deaths of three thousand Americans on September 11, 2001.

Second, the book examines the assertion that Muslims are not anti-Jewish, that they honor Jews as fellow monotheists, and that the current strife in the Middle East is political and territorial rather than religious. Again, moderate Muslims understand Islam as benevolent toward "people of the Book"—that is, believers in scripture. But those responsible for much of the carnage in the Middle East see Judaism in an entirely different light. And it is their attitude we must understand.

And third, this book challenges the claim that religious Muslims are not anti-Christian in their fight with the Israelis—that Usama bin Laden and his followers attacked the World Trade Center and the Pentagon merely because America supports the State of Israel. While Middle-Eastern Muslims are not as anti-Christian as they are anti-Jewish, this difference in the intensity of their hatred may be explainable in terms of their direct confrontation with Israelis. In Sudan and Indonesia, however, the enemies of Islam are primarily Christian.

Remember, the Jihadists this book depicts are not pasteboard Muslims—two dimensional characters constructed from select passages of the Qur'an and other Islamic scripture and served up by the *New York Times* and PBS. These guys actually exist in the world today. They have names, faces, and weapons that fire real bullets. They are our flesh-and-blood enemies; we need to understand the ideology that animates their hatred of the West.

President Bush is correct when he says that this struggle will not be resolved in the foreseeable future. Why not? Because it is about more than who controls the West Bank or the Gaza Strip. If, by some miracle we could fix the Israeli-Palestinian conflict, Usama bin Laden, hoards of Middle Eastern sheikhs, and millions of militant Muslims would still hate the United States and continue to kill Americans and other Westerners at every opportunity. They would hate us in the name of Allah and kill us in obedience to the Prophet Muhammad. And if they did so out of a radical misunderstanding of their own religion, their victims would be just as dead.

So if we are to mount a successful defense against terrorist attacks we have to be honest about our enemy. This book will provide you with a true picture of militant Islam, mostly in the words of its religious, military, and intellectual leadership.

CHAPTER ONE

Muhammad the Prophet, Messenger of Allah

In order to understand militant Islam, you have to understand the Prophet Muhammad. After all, to more than one billion followers, he is the model for all human conduct, the most perfect embodiment of the will of God (Allah). You can never grasp the meaning of Islam's continuing conflict with Christianity and Judaism unless you know the man who initiated that conflict.

In many respects, Muhammad is one of the most dramatic figures ever to occupy the world's stage. Unlike Jesus, he was both a spiritual *and* political leader, a religious prophet *and* a military conqueror. The combination has led his followers—both ancient and contemporary—to the understandable belief that an Islamic theocracy is where the world is heading, that all the earth's peoples will ultimately accept the Prophet and his version of Allah—or else.

In the seventh century, Muhammad himself led an army against the enemies of the One True God; in the twenty-first century, Usama bin Laden believes he is doing the same thing. And there have been many others in between who laid siege to the West with the express intent of imposing Islamic law (Shari'a) on the infidels. In order to put their historical mission in perspective, you need to know something of Muhammad's life—and in particular his relationship to those he called "the people of the Book "—the Jews and Christians.

Much of the current literature on Islam offers an incomplete picture of the Prophet's activities and attitudes, as well as of the contents of the Qur'an—a highly selective version for Americans, who are increasingly willing to think the best of their enemies and the worst of themselves. For example, the University of North Carolina at Chapel Hill asked its incoming freshmen to read a translation of the Qur'an that excluded key anti-Christian and anti-Jewish passages.

The following account of the Prophet's life is designed to fill in the gaps left out by other commentaries rather than to be a thorough and balanced biographical sketch. It is a narrative that attempts to shed light on the words and behavior of the Ayatollah Khomeini, Usama bin Laden, and the young Muslims who strap belts of dynamite around their waists and detonate themselves on Israeli buses.

Muhammad was born around 570 AD in the city of Mecca. He lost his parents at an early age and was raised by a rich uncle. He enjoyed all the privileges of his class until the age of 25, when he made a mistake that cost him the respect of many in the city. When the Ethiopians invaded Mecca, Muhammad, serving in his uncle's army of defenders, refused to fight, some say out of fear. As a consequence, he could no longer move among respectable people, so for a while he was a lowly shepherd.

Some Muslim historians say he became a trader—one of the chief occupations of the rich and powerful in Mecca. Others say he was an assistant to a traveling merchant. Eventually, he found a job working for a wealthy widow named Khadijah, who was fifteen years older than he was. He caught Khadijah's eye and she proposed marriage.

When Muhammad was forty years old (about 610 AD), he became moody and introspective, spending days alone with his thoughts. In this frame of mind, he was wandering in the hills when he had a vision: A figure who, according to Muhammad, identified himself as "Jibril" (Gabriel) told the terrified man that he was the last and greatest "Messenger of Allah."

The angel produced a brocaded coverlet which he ordered Muhammad to read. Since Muhammad was illiterate, the Angel hugged him four times so tightly that he couldn't breathe. At that point, Muhammad was able to recite the angel's message from memory. For the next twenty-three years, Gabriel returned to brief Muhammad concerning Allah's will; and all these briefings were passed along by Muhammad to his wife and later to his closest followers, who wrote them down. The messages comprise the Qur'an and are regarded as the word of Allah himself. Armed with this Truth, the Prophet began to preach to the people of Mecca, urging them to submit to the will of Allah.

Converts to Muhammad's new religion came slowly. The first three were Khadijah, one of the household slaves, and the slave's cousin. After three years, the converts numbered only about forty. At the time that Muhammad was slowly building his following, his own Quaraish tribe worshipped miscellaneous idols, the familiar gods of generations of Arabs, some three hundred in number. When the Prophet's followers reached a critical mass, the establishment tried to shut him down by giving him trade contracts, but he kept denouncing his tribe's religion, insisting that the world acknowledge Allah as the one true God and Muhammad as his greatest prophet. Finally, he met with tribal leaders and tried to effect a compromise—they could keep three of their gods if they would acknowledge Allah as the overarching God of all. Serge Trifkovic describes the offer in *The Sword of the Prophet:*

Attempting to sway the doubters by theological compromise, Muhammad went so far as to allow for the possibility that the three particularly well-liked Meccan deities—the moon god's daughters al-Lat, al-Uzza, and Manat—were divine beings, capable of interceding with Allah on behalf of the faithful ... Muhammad then refrained from cursing the Meccan idols but called them by the same name, "Allah," thus merging 300-odd deities at the [temple of] Kaaba into one, and calling all of them by the same name. He subsequently abrogated this section of the original Kuran, claiming that this was an interpolation of Satan—hence the "Satanic verses." (Some contemporary Muslims reject the story, but medieval Islamic scholars regarded it as authentic. It is inconceivable that Muslim chroniclers would have invented this story, which in any event underlined Muhammad's humanity.)[4]

Eventually, as Muhammad influenced more and more Meccans, the attitude of the Quraish changed from contemptuous amusement to outrage, then to fear. Too many people were converting to Islam. The old order was being undermined. Familiar household gods were no longer revered.

Muhammad's religious movement had political implications as well. As his following began to grow more rapidly, he became a greater and greater threat to the establishment, which became more and more abusive. One detractor even burst into his house in an attempt to kill him. Though he may not have known it, his days in Mecca were numbered.

In 619, he suffered two losses that left him naked to his enemies. His rich and powerful wife died, and so did his uncle—chieftain of the Quraish. Following these deaths, the Quraish leadership, as well as the rabble, escalated their mistreatment of him. He had to leave the city or risk further assassination attempts. He fled to Medina.

In so doing, he had to abandon his wealth and livelihood. Consequently, during the first years in Medina, he and his followers made ends meet by attacking and plundering desert caravans passing near the city, and their victims were mostly fellow Arabs.[5]

One of the Prophet's greatest raids occurred in 624 at Badr. Muhammad led an army of 300 against a caravan headed for Mecca, laden with riches. According to one authority,[6] the take amounted to the equivalent of $50,000. Meccans, many of whom were traders like Muhammad's wife and uncle, were angry enough to send a punitive expedition of 950 men to teach the Prophet a lesson. Instead, he taught them a lesson, losing only 14 men, killing 45 Meccans, and capturing another 70.

Among the prisoners was a Persian poet who had boasted that his folktales were more poetic than the Qur'an. Outraged at such an affront—after all, the Qur'an was spoken by Allah—the Prophet ordered the bard executed. The man begged for mercy, saying, "O Muhammad, if you kill me who will take care of my children?" to which Muhammad replied, "Hell's fire."[7] His followers, probably on his orders, also killed at least two other poets who spoke out against him.

In addition to poets, the Prophet also persecuted Jews—and for much the same reason. After he had ascended to power in Medina, he attempted to convert the Jews, from whom he had learned much. Indeed, he initially instructed Muslims to bow toward Jerusalem when they prayed and observe the Jewish Day of Atonement. He also included Jewish patriarchs in the lore of Islam.

However, his knowledge of Judaic scripture, when compared with the learning of local Jewish scholars, was so flawed that the Jews ridiculed him and rejected his claim to be God's greatest prophet. When they remained true to their ancient faith, the Prophet turned on them in anger.

Thus, in the Qur'an, Allah, as quoted by Muhammad, says:

"Because of their iniquity, we forbade the Jews good things which were formerly allowed them; because time after time they have debarred others from the path of Allah; because they practice usury—though they were forbidden it—and cheat others of their possessions." (4:16)

The Qur'an further attacks Jews by calling them blasphemers and corrupters, a people unworthy of their heritage: "Those to whom the burden of the Torah was entrusted and yet refused to bear it are like a donkey laden with books" (62:5).

Finally, when Muhammad was absolute dictator of Medina, he expelled two of the three Jewish tribes living there. They were the lucky ones.

The third tribe, the Qurayza, apparently supported Muhammad's old Meccan tribe when they fought the Muslims at the Battle of the Trench. Muhammad ordered that all the men of this tribe—some say six to eight hundred, some say nine hundred—be taken out and beheaded. After this was done, he decreed that the women and children be sold into slavery.[8]

Muslims who emphasize the kinder, gentler Islam—citing the scriptural passages in which Muhammad advocated tolerance, peace, and compassion—have a hard time dealing with this historical event. W.N. Arafat, a pro-Islam scholar with a famous last name summarizes these events as follows:

As soon as these tribes realized that Islam was being firmly established and gaining power, they adopted an actively hostile attitude and the final result of the struggle was the disappearance of these Jewish communities from Arabia proper.[9]

"The disappearance of these Jewish communities." Such euphemistic rhetoric disguises the reality.

These banishments and the beheadings of Jewish men, given the small arena in which they occurred, were the seventh-century equivalent of the driving of the Sephardic Jews from Spain and the Holocaust with its murder of millions. Certainly the goals of Muhammad and Hitler were similar: the elimination of the Jews from the community of True Believers so they would not stain the purity of a people.

Given these actions, how seriously can one take the benevolent statements of the younger Muhammad? To put the incident into perspective, suppose Jesus had armed his Apostles, recruited a few bloodthirsty followers, and beheaded all the Pharisees in Jerusalem, then sold their survivors into slavery. How seriously could a Christian—or anybody else, for that matter—take the Sermon on the Mount?

Muhammad's denunciation of Christians—as opposed to Jesus Himself, whom Muhammad praises—stems largely from his misunderstanding of the Trinity, and probably from the fact that Christians were likewise reluctant to convert to Muhammad's religion. Christian theologians developed the doctrine of the Trinity over a six-hundred-year period that included four ecumenical councils. These councils—Nicaea, Constantinople, Ephesus, and Chalcedon—are crucial to an understanding of what Christian believed at the time. In fact, the First Council of Nicaea was called in 325 to deal with the theologian Arius, who challenged the idea of the Trinity. The bishops who attended that council engaged in a lengthy debate on the subject and ultimately branded Arius a heretic.

By the time Muhammad came to the question, the Church had long since affirmed the belief that God was One, that the Father, the Son, and the Holy Spirit were three Persons in One, and that Jesus was both fully God and fully man.

In contradiction, the Qur'an—supposedly composed by Allah and conveyed to the world through Muhammad—informs the Islamic faithful that Jesus is not Divine and that Christians worship three gods, a position the Church had repeatedly denounced. This misconception is made explicit in Sura 4, verse 171.

> The Messiah, Jesus the son of Mary, was no more than God's [Allah's] apostle ...So believe in God [Allah] and his apostles and do not say: "Three." Forbear, and it shall be better for you. God is but one God. God forbid that he should have a son!

Whatever the origin of his misconception, Muhammad—while depicting Jesus as a star of lesser magnitude—sees Christians as polytheists and therefore the enemies of Allah, since they are believers in false gods and hence blasphemers against the One True God.

Umar, the second in succession after the Prophet's death and Muhammad's close associate, quotes him as saying, "I will expel the polytheists from the Arabian peninsula." (Ironically, Muhammad meant Jews as well as Christians, since, after the Jewish elders rejected him, the Prophet said their ancestors slew their prophets and worshipped golden idols.)

Indeed, while the early segments of the Qur'an are benevolent toward both Jews and Christians, the later segments contain harsh and vindictive anti-Jewish and anti-Christian statements—all uttered by the same Allah. So the Prophet of so-called moderate Muslims is a gentle man, full of love and tolerance for "the people of the Book." But the Prophet of the militant Muslims is fiercely anti-Jewish and anti-Christian, a leader who calls on his followers to shun the enemies of Allah and finally to drive them from the Middle East.

It is no accident that Usama bin Laden, following an attack on

Americans in Saudi Arabia, should praise the terrorists who killed Christians and exhort such holy warriors to continue their assault on "the Zionists and Crusaders." The subtitle of bin Laden's militant endorsement of holy war is pointed: "I Will Expel the Polytheists from the Arabian Peninsula"—the words of Muhammad himself.

Millions of Muslims have taken up this cry, and those Westerners who want to seek the origins of the current violence and bloodletting, need look no further than the Qur'an and the life of Allah's Messenger, the Prophet Muhammad.

CHAPTER TWO

Jihad! Jihad!

It is particularly instructive to see how American Muslim groups, Washington politicians, and the media define "Jihad"—an Arab word that Americans have learned through bitter experience over the past several years. Now opinion makers are ordering us to relearn the meaning, "since Islam is a religion of peace."

Those who still believe that "Jihad" means "holy war" are told they haven't read the right books or visited the right websites. Jihad is not crashing airplanes into skyscrapers or suicide bombings but a spiritual struggle that takes place in the inner sanctum of the soul.

One Islamic website (www.submission.org) defines the word this way:

Jihad has a great significance in the lives of Muslims ...Like any language, Arabic has unique words which have a particular meaning which cannot be translated precisely. The best translation known for such a word is the following: a sincere and noticeable effort (for good): an all true and unselfish striving for spiritual good.[10]

Jihad as presented in the Quran and any of the other [Islamic] scriptures implies the striving of spiritual good. This Jihad particularly involves change in one's self and mentality. It may concern the sacrifice of material property, social class and even emotional comfort solely for the salvation and worship of God ALONE. As a result, one who practices Jihad will gain tremendously in the Hereafter.[11]

Did St. Francis of Assisi, Mother Teresa, and Martin Luther King, Jr. "practice Jihad," or at least some rough Christian approximation? The following description suggests that they did.

Examples of this Jihad would be to exceed in the sincere act of good deeds (to frequent the mosques that worship God alone more often; to study the scripture in detail, to help the poor and the orphans, to stand for people's right for freedom, be equitable, never bear false testimony, frequent and stay in good terms with friends and neighbors, etc.) and the restraining of the doing of sins (to commit adultery, to steel [sic], to lie, to cheat, to insult people, to gossip, etc.)[12]

This definition extends the meaning to include almost any thoughtful behavior—whether performing ethical acts or refraining from the commission of crimes. It means lending your neighbors a cup of sugar or keeping quiet about their marital difficulties.

Toward the end of this homily, the anonymous author does admit that "Jihad" might have some connection with war.

Jihad may also reflect the war aspects in Islam (Submission). The fighting of a war in the name of justice or Islam, to deter an aggressor, for self defense, and/or to establish justice or freedom to practice religion, would also be considered a Jihad.[13]

The rest of the article is devoted to repeated denials that a Jihad can be a "holy war":

"Jihad is anything but a holy war; the media and the public misunderstand this."[14]

"To Islam (Submission), war is unholy, Jihad must mean anything but holy war."[15]

"The other condition and perhaps the most important and often confused as a holy war, is a war in the name of God which actually means in the cause of God as God does not encourage war but rather encourages peace whenever possible."[16]

In Brief; the meaning the media give to this word (Jihad) is false. This word does not mean a holy war, for there is nothing holy about a war in Islam (submission).[17]

Another contemporary Islamic site—*About Islam and Muslims* —has this to say about "Jihad."

The word Jihad means striving. In its primary sense it is an inner thing, within self, to rid it from debased actions or inclinations, and exercise constancy and perseverance in achieving a higher moral standard. Since Islam is not confined to the boundaries of the individual but extends to the welfare of society and humanity in general, an individual cannot keep improving himself/herself in isolation from what happens in their community or in the world at large, hence the Quranic instruction to the Islamic nation to take as a duty "to enjoin good and forbid evil."[18]

This commentary likewise rejects the idea that Jihad is a threat to other religions.

> Jihad is not a declaration of war against other religions and certainly not against Christians and Jews as some media and political circles want it to be perceived. Islam does not fight other religions. Christians and Jews are considered as fellow inheritors of the Abrahamic traditions by Muslims, worshipping the same God and following the tradition of Abraham.[19]

These statements contain an incomplete definition of the word. As already noted, the Qur'an and Muhammad pay lip service to the historical connections between Islam, Judaism, and Christianity, with Moses and Jesus treated as prophets of Islam (though not as great as Muhammad himself). These conciliatory statements were made early in his life, when the Prophet was trying to convert Jews and Christians to Islam. When he became absolute ruler of Medina, his comments on these other religions were far more hostile and threatening.

Indeed, later Muslim scripture specifically condemns the Jews as unworthy of their heritage and orthodox Christians as idolaters, guilty of the sin of "shirk" (worshipping gods other than Allah). Instead of coming to terms directly and honestly with these passages—thereby revealing the dark side of Islam and Jihad—the author offers a vague mea culpa that includes all religions.

> We have to acknowledge again, for the sake of honesty, that historically all traditions, Muslim, Christian, Jew as well as others, had their lapses in honestly following the valued ideals of their religions and philosophies. We all make mistakes and we still do. Muslims are no exception, and time and again religion was exploited by ambitious tyrants or violated by ignorant mobs.[20]

This equation of Islam with Judaism and Christianity suggests that the attack on the World Trade Center and the suicide bombings in the Middle East were carried out by Muslims who either didn't understand their faith or couldn't live up to its ideals.

The leaders of Jihad are by no means mere ambitious tyrants, and they are hardly ignorant of their faith. They can justify everything they say and do by the words and deeds of the Prophet.

Make no mistake: To many millions of Muslims throughout the world, "Jihad" means "holy war." Anyone who believes otherwise will surely think differently after reading the statements of the angry Muslim sheikhs, clerics, and commentators quoted in the pages to come. And there are more quotations where these came from—as many as the sands of the desert.

The entire Middle East is inflamed by this bloodthirsty rhetoric—much of it echoing Muhammad's seventh-century call to drive Christians and Jews from the Arabian peninsula. In the next chapter are just a few examples to show how those other Muslims define "Jihad."

CHAPTER THREE

Jihad for the Clerics and their Followers

I n a shrill sermon broadcast live on the official Palestinian Authority TV, a Muslim cleric, after denouncing the Jews in particular, called for Jihad against both Jews and Christians:

Have no mercy on the Jews, no matter where they are, in any country. Fight them, wherever you are. Wherever you meet them, kill them. Wherever you are, kill those Jews and those Americans who are like them—and those who stand by them—they are all in one trench, against the Arabs and the Muslims—because they have established Israel here, in the beating heart of the Arab world, in Palestine. They created it to be the out-post of their civilization—and the vanguard of their army, and to be the sword of the West and the crusaders, hanging over the necks of the monotheists, the Muslims in these lands. They wanted the Jews to be their spearhead ...

Let us put our trust in Allah, close ranks, and unite our words, and the slogan of us all should be, "Jihad! Jihad! For the sake of Palestine, and for the sake of Jerusalem and Al-Aqsa.[21]

An Iraqi sheikh ("sheikh" can mean religious leader as well as tribal chieftain) discussed the political situation in the context of Ramadan, the holiest month of the Muslim year, during which, according to a Muslim website, "...Muslims fast during the day-light hours and in the evening eat small meals and visit with friends and family. It is a time of worship and contemplation. A time to strengthen family and communities." Consider what this sheikh wants Muslim families and communities to contemplate:.

We know and believe, Oh Allah, that these hardships are a test for us and for our patience. We tell you, Oh Allah, that we are patient ...and we will fight them with all kinds of weapons. Jihad, Jihad, Jihad, Jihad. Oh nation of the Koran, the nation of Muhammad, Oh Muslims: Jihad for the cause of Allah, and for defending Muhammad's holiness. Whoever does not defend Muhammad and the Koran, will not smell the aroma of par-adise forever. What is the meaning of this peaceful slumber?

What is the meaning of this numbness? What is the meaning of these hollow statements that do not rise to the level of the needed responsibility? Today, after the capture of Jerusalem, and after the infidels defiled the Arabian Peninsula and are threatening Arabs and Muslims, the holy places, and especially Iraq—Jihad has become an obligation of every individual Muslim [Fardh 'Ayn]. Anyone who does not comply, will find himself lost [in hell], side by side with Haman, Pharaoh, and their soldiers.

These are not just words of a sermon delivered from the pulpit of a mosque with enthusiasm, they are religious law.

Oh Allah, let the infidels fight each other, and dry their blood in their veins. Send your soldiers against them; Allah, shake the ground under their feet; Allah, destroy their fleet and their weapons; fight their soldiers; Allah, and plant fear in them; Oh, Allah, confuse their words; Allah, make them prey to the Muslims; Allah, avenge Muslims' blood from them ...Oh Allah, reduce the word of the infidels, and heighten the word of the believers. Oh Allah, raise the banner of monotheism, raise the slogan of monotheism ..."Allah Akbar" to the criminals; "Allah Akbar" to America; "Allah Akbar" to Britain ...Oh Allah do not let the Jews or the crusaders overcome the Muslims ...Allah, help the Jihad warriors everywhere ...Oh Allah, for Thee we fight, we kill and are killed. Allah will settle His account with you, Bush! Allah will settle His account with you, Ariel Sharon! Allah will settle His account with you, Britons! Allah will settle His account with you, enemies of Allah....Our dead for the cause of Allah are Shuhada [martyrs] in paradise, while their dead are in hell....[22]

The rhetoric becomes shriller and shriller, ending in wild vituperation and a call to arms. Reading this sermon, it is impossible to accept the proposition that this brand of Islam is a religion of peace. Clearly its darker side foments fierce religious warfare. Another sheikh is equally shrill:.

Blessings for whoever assaulted a soldier ...Blessings for whoever has raised his sons on the education of Jihad and Martyrdom; blessings for whoever has saved a bullet in order to stick it in the head of a Jew.

Sheikh Isma'il Aal Ghadwan, in a live broadcast on Palestinian TV, delivered a sermon, excerpts of which are printed below. In his homily, which is little more than an exhortation to kill Jews, he specifically mentions the promise of the Prophet that martyrs will be serviced by black-eyed virgins.

...It is the duty of the Islamic nation to open the gates of Jihad, where its strength and honor lie. We are a nation that was given Islam and Jihad by Allah....

When the enemies of Allah, the Jews, may Allah curse them, mutilate [the bodies] and chop off organs—these organs will serve as evidence for our sons and brothers for whom Paradise in the high heavens is a place of refuge. [Even when] a martyr's organs are being chopped off, and he turns into torn organs that spread all over, in order to meet Allah, Muhammad, and his friends, it would not be considered a loss ...

Oh believing brothers, we do not feel a loss ...The martyr, if he meets Allah, is forgiven with the first drop of blood; he is saved from the torments of the grave; he sees his place in Paradise; he is saved from the Great Horror [of the day of judgment]; he is given 72 black-eyed women; he vouches for 70 of his family to be accepted to Paradise; he is crowned with the Crown of glory, whose precious stone is better than all of this world and what is in it ...

A sermon by a Muslim cleric, broadcast over Palestinian TV, addresses the question of educating Muslim children. What should they be taught? How should Palestinians prepare them for the future? The answer is chilling.

Even if they slaughter all of the Palestinian people and the only survivors will be one single Palestinian baby girl and one Palestinian baby boy, the baby boy will marry the baby girl and they will give birth to the one who will liberate Jerusalem from the defilement of the Jews.

We must prepare ourselves in accordance with the religion of Allah and the Law of Allah. We must educate our children on the love of Jihad for the sake of Allah and the love of fighting for the sake of Allah.[25]

Nurtured on such rhetoric, it is small wonder that Palestinian children become suicide bombers, with the outspoken approval of their parents. If you don't think this kind of rhetoric has an impact on Muslim families, read what one mother, Umm Nidal, had to say about the death of her son, Muhammad Farhat, a suicide bomber.

When asked how her son decided to blow himself up, she replied: "Jihad is a [religious] commandment imposed upon us. We must instill this idea in our sons' souls, all the time ...What we see every day—massacres, destruction, bombing [of] homes—strengthened, in the souls of my sons, especially Muhammad, the love of Jihad and martyrdom."

And did she have any role in nurturing such an idea?

"Allah be praised," she replied. "I am a Muslim and I believe in Jihad. Jihad is one of the elements of the faith, and this is what encouraged me to sacrifice Muhammad in Jihad for the sake of Allah. My son was not destroyed, he is not dead; he is living a happier life than I. Had my thoughts been limited to this world, I would not sacrifice Muhammad.

"I am a compassionate mother to my children, and they are compassionate towards me and take care of me. Because I love my son, I encouraged him to die a martyr's death for the sake of Allah. Jihad is a religious obligation incumbent upon us, and we must carry it out. I sacrificed Muhammad as part of my obligation."

Particularly chilling is this woman's description of her last encounters with her son. It is inconceivable that the most patriotic Gold Star Mother in America could have entertained such feelings about a son whose overriding purpose was to get himself killed in battle. Clearly the religious commitment to Jihad overrode her instincts as a mother—and in a way that could only be termed unnatural.

She tells of how he tried several times to create an opportunity for martyrdom and how he called his rifle "my bride." Then she tells of their last meeting and how he finally got his wish:

On the day of the operation, he came to me and told me: "Now, mother, I am setting out for my operation." He prepared for the operation two days in advance, when the video was filmed. He asked me to be photographed with him, and during the filming he brandished his gun. I personally asked to make the film so as to remember.

He set out to carry out the operation, and when he got to the area he spent the night with his friends there. I was in contact with him and I asked him about his morale. He told me he was very happy. Indeed, I saw his face happier than I had ever seen it.

He set out for his operation with cold nerves, completely calm and confident, as if convinced that the operation would succeed.

But I worried and feared greatly that the operation would not succeed, and that he would be arrested. I prayed for him when he left the house and asked Allah to make his operation a success and give him martyrdom. When he entered the settlement, his brothers in the military wing [of Hamas] informed me that he had managed to infiltrate it. Then I began to pray to Allah for him.

I prayed from the depths of my heart that Allah would cause the success of his operation. I asked Allah to give me 10 [Israelis] for Muhammad, and Allah granted my request and Muhammad made his dream come true, killing 10 Israeli settlers and soldiers. Our God honored him even more, in that there were many Israelis wounded.

When the operation was over, the media broadcast the news. Then Muhammad's brother came to me and informed me of his martyrdom. I began to cry, 'Allah is the greatest,' and prayed and thanked Allah for the success of the operation. I began to utter cries of joy and we declared that we were happy. The young people began to fire into the air out of joy over the success of the operation, as this is what we had hoped for him.

After this martyrdom [operation], my heart was peaceful about Muhammad. I encouraged all my sons to die a martyr's death, and I wish this even for myself. After all this, I prepared myself to receive the body of my son, the pure shahid, in order to look upon him one last time and accept the well-wishers who [came] to us in large numbers and participated in our joy over Muhammad's martyrdom....[26]

Others revere their martyrs, but not in the same way that this Muslim mother does. In the first place, from its beginnings, the

Christian Church forbade *deliberate* martyrdom, which is regarded as suicide. Some Muslim scholars claim that suicide bombings are likewise contrary to Muslim law. If so, a growing number of the followers of Islam, including this mother, know little or nothing about their faith.

CHAPTER FOUR

Jihad Among the Learned and Elite

Defenders of Islam have argued that the ideas and sentiments expressed in such sermons are analogous to those voiced by backwoods Christian preachers who scream and rage to whip their congregations into an emotional frenzy, that thoughtful Muslims neither feel so strongly nor think so heretically. In other words, it is the difference between Elmer Gantry and the dean of the Harvard Divinity School.

Such comparisons do not apply. Islam is not Christianity, and the Middle East is not the United States of America. The split between "radical Islam" and "moderate Islam" is not one of class and education so much as one of doctrinal strictness. Militant Islam also has its intellectuals. Numerous advocates of Jihad have even been educated in the West, and are highly learned. Consider two examples:

The first is from the online magazine Al-Ansar, a pro-Al-Quaida publication. This sophisticated article explores the Muslim belief in predestination, particularly as it relates to Jihad. The question it raises and answers: If the defeat of Christians and Jews at the hands of Allah and his earthly warriors is predetermined, if Islam is predestined to rule the world, why should current Muslims—against overwhelming odds—fight, and commit suicide? This article—quoting the Qur'an ("Allah will torture them at your hands")—uses the doctrine of predestination as a means of furthering the cause of the struggle against the infidels.

> Regardless of the norms of "humanist" belief, which sees destroying the infidel countries as a tragedy requiring us to show some conscientious empathy and ...an atmosphere of sadness for the loss that is to be caused to human civilization—an approach that does not distinguish between believer and infidel ...—I would like to stress that annihilating the infidels is an inarguable fact, as this is the [divine] decree of fate....
>
> When the Koran places these tortures [to be inflicted on the infidels] in the solid framework of reward and punishment ...it seeks to root this predestined fact in the consciousness of the Muslim group, asserting that the infidels will be annihilated, so as to open a window of hope to the Muslim group....[27]

The article goes on to say that the "fact" non-Muslim nations will certainly be annihilated does not mean that the Muslim world should sit idly by and wait for Allah to fulfill this prophecy. Sometimes Allah helps those who help themselves.

> When Allah told us of the certainty of the annihilation of the infidels, he did not do so using ambiguous concepts. He clarified that this would be achieved in one of two ways: by means of a direct act of Allah ...or by means of the Muslim group, which would, in accordance with Islamic commandment, serve as an implement for carrying out [the divine decree], as it is said:

"...Allah will torture them [the infidels] Himself or at our hands."
(Koran 9:52)[28]

Remember that the infidels whom Allah will torture are Christians and Jews and that, for many Muslims, Islam is predestined to destroy Judaism and Christianity. And how can the Muslim world assist Allah in this great undertaking? Again the Qur'an supplies an answer: "Fight them and Allah will torture them at your hands." The article then specifies precisely how the fight should be conducted.

> The question now on the agenda is, how is the torture Allah wants done at our hands to be carried out? ...This torture will not, in any way, be carried out by means of preaching [Da'wa], because preaching is activity of exposure, aimed at clarifying the truth in a way that makes it more easily acceptable. Preaching has nothing to do with torture; Jihad is the way of torturing [the infidels] at our hands.
>
> By means of Jihad, Allah tortures them with killing; by means of Jihad, Allah tortures them with injury; by means of Jihad, Allah tortures them with loss of property; by means of Jihad, Allah tortures them with loss of ruling. Allah tortures them by means of Jihad—that is, with heated war that draws its fire from the military front ...[29]

The second example is from an interview with a noted Islamic scholar. Al-Jazeera, the Qatar-based TV network, sponsors a weekly program on the Islamic religion. Recently, the subject was Muhammad as the quintessential example of the Jihad warrior. The guest was Sheikh Yussef Al-Qaradhawi, a recognized authority on Islam and head of the "Muslim Brotherhood" movement.

Sheikh Al-Qaradhawi began by reminding his audience that "Allah established in the life of the Prophet Muhammad general, eternal, and all inclusive characteristics, and he gave every human being the possibility to imitate him and take his life as a model." Thus, the sheikh argues, that "...Allah has ...made the prophet Muhammad into an epitome for religious warriors [Mujahideen] since he ordered Muhammad to fight for religion ..." (Jesus, he points out, is a poor model for the Christian soldier, since He never went to war.)[30]

The sheikh cites the fact that Muhammad did not fight during his earlier days in Mecca as an example of restraint. However, he says that given current circumstances, the Prophet's example in Medina is a better model.

> On the other hand, there are some things that cannot wait; for instance, when the land of the Muslims is being invaded. When that happens, we do not say "let's wait, we will surrender to them and only then [we shall see]"...no! In that case, Islam requires that the people of the invaded land will fight the invaders ...and following them, their neighbors. And if this is not enough, all the Muslims [must enlist for this purpose]. Hence, a problem like the current Intifada and the Palestinian problem is one that cannot wait; the nation must fight and defend itself and not allow the invader to ruin the land ...."[31]

The sheikh argues that the Palestinians were like prisoners and therefore were not required to "fulfill the duty of Jihad," but that the rest of Islam is obliged to come to the aid of the captive: "...it is obvious that when it is the homeland that was captured, the land of The Prophet's Ascension to Heaven [Jerusalem], the land of the prophets and holy places, and the first direction of prayer [Qibla]—the Muslims around the world must make ever effort to save the Al-Aqsa Mosque and to help the residents [of

Palestine], since the Al-Aqsa Mosque is not the property of the Palestinian people only, but of each and every Muslim ...

The sheikh describes the preparation for Jihad, as exemplified by Muhammad himself. He begins by differentiating between two kinds of Jihad—when Islam is the invader and when Islam is being invaded: "The repulsing Jihad takes place when your land is being invaded and conquered ...[in that case you must] repulse [the invader] to the best of your ability; if you kill him he will end up in hell, and if he kills you, you become a martyr [Shahid] ..."[33]

After outlining the ways the Prophet prepared his men for Jihad, he points out that the loss to Israel in 1967 can be attributed to poor preparation—and in particular a lack of religious indoctrination. The troops were not told that they fought for Islam and that if they died in battle, they would be rewarded in heaven.

> Officers stated that we had vast amounts of weapons but we did not provide the warrior with mental preparation. We did not prepare him to fight for religious belief and for defending religious sanctuaries. We are the oppressed, and the duty is on us. He who got killed is a [Shahid] in heaven ...the first assignment is to prepare the hero who is willing to put his life in his own hands for Allah's sake, and he who does not care whether he encounters death or death encounters him ...

When questioned, the Sheikh repeated a position he had taken all along, that Palestinian "suicide bombers" were not suicides at all but warriors in battle:

> He kills the enemy while taking self-risk, similarly to what Muslims did in the past ... He wants to scare his enemies, and the religious authorities have permitted this. They said that if

he causes the enemy both sorrow and fear of Muslims ...he is permitted to risk himself and even get killed.

He ends the interview with a plea to keep the fight going: "At the very least, the Intifada [uprising] must go on, intensify, become more sophisticated, and broaden its base. And we must take whatever we can from the current rulers who are incapable of fighting...."[36]

What Sheikh Al-Qaradhawi is prescribing here (offering Muhammad as his guide chief exemplum) is an increase in the terrorist measures taken by Palestinians in Jerusalem—and the suicide bombings in particular. He calls for an escalation of the violence and a simultaneous program of indoctrination that teaches soldiers the war they are fighting is in defense of Islam and that death in battle in rewarded in heaven, while the enemy dead are punished in hell for attacking Muslims.

The tone of the sheikh's discourse is less strident than many of the sermons of his fellow believers. Here, he is the Islamic scholar, sharing his wisdom with his audience in measured language. However, his message is essentially the same as that of his shriller brothers: In order to drive out the infidels, Muslims must be prepared to die for Allah in all-out Jihad.

By early 2001, the Arab media in the Middle East and elsewhere were exploring the theological implications of suicide bombings, printing both sides of the question. For example, the Mufti of Saudi Arabia believed such actions were contrary to the Islamic faith: "I am not aware of anything in the religious law regarding killing oneself in the heart of the enemy's ranks, or what is called 'suicide.' This is not a part of Jihad, and I fear that it is merely killing oneself. Although the Koran permits and even demands the killing of the enemy, this must be done in ways that do not contradict the Shari'a [Islamic Religious Law]."[37]

However, other religious authorities disputed this interpretation.

- Sheikh Hamed Al-Bitawi, head of the Palestinian Islamic Scholars Association, said: "Jihad is a collective duty [Fardh Kifaya] ... However, if infidels conquer even an inch of the Muslim's land, as happened with the occupation of Palestine by the Jews, then Jihad becomes an individual duty [Fardh 'Ayn]," and therefore, suicide attacks are permissible.[38]

- Dr. Abd Al-Aziz Al-Rantisi, a leader of the Hamas, offered a slightly different defense of suicide bombing: "[S]uicide depends on volition. If the martyr intends to kill himself because he is tired of life—it is suicide. However, if he wants to sacrifice his soul in order to strike the enemy and to be rewarded by Allah—he is considered a martyr [rather than someone who committed suicide]. We have no doubt that those carrying out these operations are martyrs."[39]

- Sheikh Yussuf Al-Qaradhawi concurred: "These operations are the supreme form of Jihad for the sake of Allah, and a type of terrorism that is allowed by the Shari'a."[40] In an interview with an Egyptian newspaper, Al-Qaradhawi elaborates on the point: "While someone who commits suicide has lost hope with himself and with the spirit of Allah, the *Mujahid* [Jahid warrior] is full of hope with regard to Allah's spirit and mercy. He fights his enemy and the enemy of Allah with this new weapon, which destiny has put in the hands of the weak, so that they would fight against the evil of the strong and arrogant. The Mujahid becomes a 'human bomb' that blows up at a specific place and time, in the midst of the enemies of Allah and the homeland, leaving them helpless in the face of the brave Shahid [Martyr] who ...sold his soul to Allah, and sought the Shahada [Martyrdom] for the sake of Allah."[41]

- The Sheikh of Al-Azhar, Muhammad Sayyed Tantawi, the leading Sunni Muslim authority in Egypt, defines a new right, one that political activists in the United States have yet to discover. Tantawi is quoted as saying: "It is every Muslim, Palestinian and Arab's right to blow himself up in the heart of Israel, an honorable death is better than a life of humiliation. All religious laws have demanded the use of force against the enemy and fighting against those who stand by Israel; there is no escape from fighting, from Jihad, and from [self]-defense, and whoever refrains from such things is not a believer."[42] Later Sheikh Tantawi would modify his position: "[T]he Palestinian youth who bomb themselves amongst people who fight against them, are considered martyrs ...On the other hand, if they bomb themselves amongst babies, women, and elderly, they are not considered martyrs."[43]

- The scholars of Al-Azhar and the 'Al-Azhar Center for Islamic Research published an opinion on the subject: "He who sacrifices himself [a fidaai] is he who gives his soul in order to come closer to Allah....When the Muslims are attacked in their homes and their land is robbed, the Jihad for Allah turns into an individual duty. In this case, operations of martyrdom become a primary obligation and Islam's highest form of Jihad." The opinion also endorses the idea of children as suicide bombers: "[T]he participation of Palestinian children and youths in the Intifada is a type of Jihad

...when Jihad becomes an individual duty, all Muslims must join in, and children must go [to battle], even without asking permission from their parents. Those who sell their soul to Allah are the avant garde of the Shahids [martyrs] in Allah's eyes, and they express the revival of the nation, its steadfastness in struggle, and the fact of its being alive and not dead."[44]

• Saddam Hussein himself entered the debate, predictably in favor of suicide bombing. His reasoning is at least as subtly sophistical as that of the sheikhs and scholars in the region: "The martyrdom of those who are fighting for Palestine, does not mean giving up on life, but rather, protecting its meaning. It is martyrdom in order to [guarantee] life for the coming generations. It does not mean giving up life out of desperation. It is the height of optimism and the most exact expression of life."[45]

• In replying to those who want to make a distinction between military and civilian casualties of suicide bombings, Dr. Muhammad Kamal Al-Din Al-Imam—lecturing on Islamic law to the Alexandria [Egypt] law faculty—said such a distinction does not exist: "The [Israeli] society as a whole attacks the land of Palestine. They are all armed, they are all part of a military force, they are all recruited. They came from various countries in order to occupy someone else's land. Can someone who has committed such a crime be treated as a civilian?!! Israel is a Dar Harb [an area not under Israel's control] and its citizens are considered aggressors and plunderers ...These [Muslim warriors] by no means commit suicide. Each part in their bodies speaks [the language] of Martyrdom for the sake of Allah." In challenging the more moderate Shari'a authorities, he offers another reason for allowing suicide bombing, one that appeals to Muslim pride: "The religious authorities have allowed [even] the killing of a Muslim, if the heretic enemy is using him as a shield and there is no other way of killing this heretic, but to kill the Muslim along with him ...[I]n such a case, the killing of the Muslim is permitted."[46]

- Dr. Muhammad Hassan Abd Al-Khaleq, a lecturer in Hebrew, claimed that his knowledge of Jews gave him a special insight into these suicide bombers. His knowledge included the canard that Jews use the blood of non-Jews to make Passover bread: "Anyone who forbids these [suicide] operations does not know anything about these Jews. How can anyone forbid the killing of people who believe that stealing and killing is part of their false faith? The Jews have interpreted the Commandment 'Thou shall not kill' as 'Thou shall not kill a Jews.' ...Many cases of inhuman acts of murder carried out by them for religious motives have been registered in history, like the murder of a Christian priest and the collecting of his blood in order to make of it a Passover matzah. This happened at the beginning of the nineteenth-century in Damascus and has been proven to be true ..."[47]

It is difficult to reconcile the sermons, articles, and interviews quoted above with the definition of "Jihad" as given by moderate Muslims. Clearly some Islamic experts view the idea of a "holy war" in the same way Muslim critics in the United States view it—as contrary to the faith, an emphasis on the wrong section of the Qur'an and the later words of the Prophet. However, the others understand the word "Jihad" differently.

CHAPTER FIVE

Militant Islam and the Jews

Jews in the Middle East understand better than anyone what Jihad means to their surrounding neighbors. They are daily victims of the violence it generates. When they are not killing Jews in the streets of Israel, militant Muslims are parading their hatred in other ways.

Take, for example, their high-decibel rhetoric. Most Americans are repelled by such anti-Jewish diatribes, seeing them as one more example of the anti-Semitism that has plagued the world since the Middle Ages and which led, in time, to the Holocaust. Historically, Muslim hatred of Jews is something more than mere ethnic bigotry—by itself an extremely dangerous phenomenon. In Islam, anti-Jewish attitudes have their roots in Islamic scripture and, more particularly, in the words and actions of the Prophet.

As noted in Chapter Two, Muhammad expelled two Jewish tribes from Medina, then beheaded all the men of a third tribe, and sold their survivors into slavery. His reasons: The Jews had scorned his botched account of Jewish history and had refused to convert en masse to Islam. At that point, when he was absolute dictator of the city, he put aside the pretense of tolerance and wielded his new-found power to win converts with the sword. Along with the Prophet's statement that he would "expel the polytheists from the Arabian peninsula," his treatment of the Jewish tribes in Medina has become a paradigm for latter-day Muslim leaders.

To be sure, the political plight of the Palestinians has appealed to Islam worldwide. Muslims everywhere tend to view Israel as a state created by force and theft, carved out of Islamic territory with the help of Western Christian nations—principally the United States and Britain.

But Muslim support for Palestine extends beyond mere sympathy for a "displaced people." Palestinians belong to Allah, and Muslims regard the Jews as the oldest enemies of the Prophet. Arab Muslims attack Jews with a hatred that can only be described as wildly, passionately religiose—a rage that can't be dispelled by soothing words or hair-splitting compromise. The lion will lie down by the lamb sooner than these Muslims will live side by side with Jews.

To understand just how strong Muslim hatred of Jews can be, consider the following commentary by Mustafa Bakri, an editor of the Egyptian opposition newspaper Al-Usbu. He describes a dream in which he is asked to serve as a bodyguard for Ariel Sharon, Prime Minister of Israel:

After a short while, the pig landed; his face was diabolical, a murderer; his hands soiled with the blood of women and children. A criminal who should be executed in the town square. Should I remain silent as many others did? Should I guard this butcher on my homeland's soil? All of a sudden, I forgot everything: the past and the future, my wife and my children and I decided to do it. I pulled my gun and aimed it at the cowardly pig's head. I emptied all the bullets and screamed: blood-vengeance for the [Egyptian] POWs, blood-vengeance for the martyrs. The murderer collapsed under my feet. I breathed a sigh of relief. I realized the meaning of virility, and of self-sacrifice. The criminal died. I stepped on the pig's head with my shoes and screamed from the bottom of my heart: Long live Egypt, long live Palestine, Jerusalem will never die and never will the honor of the nation be lost. I kept screaming at the top of my lungs until my wife put her hand upon me. I woke up from the most beautiful dream and decided not to surrender to humiliation.[48]

This dream—if it is not an invention designed to lend color to an anti-Jewish editorial—shows just how deep the hatred runs in Bakri's subconscious. That he chose to write about it without shame or apology suggests the degree to which he believes Egyptian Muslims in large numbers share his fantasy.

Bakri's editorial was published, not in Iraq or Iran, but in Egypt—the land of peacemaker Anwar Sadat. In other nations, the hatred is even more militant. An Iraqi sheikh reminds his audience that the Qur'an describes the Jews as animals:

Allah has described [the Jews] as apes and pigs, the calf-worshipers, idol-worshipers . . .they have said that we are cockroaches and ants and that they should kill us, but we approach them with the words of Allah: ". . .Whoever wants to save himself, should enter to the true religion—Islam—and repent, and then there will be no problems between him and us, our rights will be his and his obligations will be ours. However, he who came to this land as an invader and did not enter the religion of Allah, should go back to the place he came from, or else our spears will reach him, Allah willing."[49]

Many Americans still tend to believe that fanaticism is characteristic of the uneducated and powerless—the Ku Klux Klan, the American Nazi party, the Black Panthers, the followers of the Reverend Jim Jones. Nazism and Communism should have taught us better. Both of these political systems produced their own philosophers, scientists, and artists—people who should have known better but whose minds became the handservants of ideology.

The same is true of militant Islam. The uneducated mobs in the streets of Tehran, Baghdad, and Bombay have their counterparts in the intellectual and professional circles of the Middle East, East Jerusalem, and even the United States. Yet the level of discourse among the Muslim intelligentsia is hardly more rational than that of the rabble-rousers in the streets.

For example, *Al-Jazeera,* the government-controlled daily newspaper in Saudi Arabia, recently published an article by Dr. Muhammad bin Sad Al-Shwey'ir, editor-in-chief of the *Islamic Research Journal* of the Islamic Clerics Association of Saudi Arabia. Given his credentials, it seems reasonable to assume that Dr. Shwey'ir is a distinguished scholar whose research is of the highest quality.

However, an examination of his work proves otherwise. He is one more example of the degree to which Muslim ideology—grounded in blind hatred—corrupts reason, judgment, and integrity. Among other things, he repeats as fact the anti-Semitic folk tales that have haunted Western Jews for centuries—old and vicious superstitions that Christians have long since discarded.

First, there is the story of the Passover bread.

> Christian Europe showed enmity toward the Jews when it transpired that their rabbis craftily hunt anyone walking alone, [tempting] him to enter their house of worship. Then they take his blood to use for baked goods for their holidays, as part of their ritual. Often this deed was uncovered even in the Arab and Islamic countries that protected them.[50]

This slander has its origins in the Middle Ages, and a similar story is even found in Chaucer's *Canterbury Tales.* In modern times, it has died out, chiefly because there is no evidence to support such an outrageous claim and because it makes absolutely no sense theologically. However, the Muslims have revived it to discredit the Jews among their own people, as well as among Christians.

Dr. Al-Shwey'ir also commends the *Protocols of the Elders of Zion*, whose authenticity he accepts without question. In particular, he discusses the "24th protocol":

> ...it represents the goal towards which the Jews strive with their tactics, their false media, and their treachery. The free world must take notice—primarily the West and America, where the intentions of the Jews have been revealed—as they gnaw away at the societies like the worm gnaws away at the wood until it is entirely consumed before signs [of the damage] are [visible]. [The West and America] must awaken, and must support the Muslims against them [i.e., the Jews] before it is too late.[51]

The 24th Protocol discusses the steps necessary to enthrone a Jewish king, a descendant of David, to rule the world. According to the protocols, this is the final stage of the grand strategy developed by "Jewish Masons" to corrupt and destroy all non-Jewish societies, then to set up a world government of their own. Ironically, the militant Muslims of the Middle East often refer to a time when the entire world will submit to Islam or be slaughtered. This day will come, they believe, when the Caliphate (rule by caliphs) is reinstated. The similarities of these visions—the one a forgery, the other a part of Islamic lore—are striking.

Dr. Al-Shwey'ir resurrects yet another moribund anti-Semitic myth in the following passage:

> Do the Americans—both rulers and ruled—realize that these are the thoughts and conspiracies [of the Jews] toward the human race? If not, they must take another look at what their

president [sic] Benjamin Franklin said when he warned the American people of the danger posed by the Jews, in his speech at the conference convened to declare the American Constitution in 1789....[52]

Dr. Al-Shwey'ir is not the only Middle Eastern Muslim to repeat this fabrication. Several others have done so. Note that no one comes up with the precise quotation, though a well-annotated edition of the proceedings of the Constitutional Convention is readily available.

Franklin never made such a statement.

He was a friend of the Jews. In fact, he and other non-Jews raised money to help a Jewish congregation in Philadelphia pay off a substantial debt.

Because of his advanced degree and his reputation as a scholar, Dr. Al-Shwey'ir has been able to lend substantial credibility to a number of anti-Semitic falsehoods that have long ago been dismissed by educated Westerners. In so doing, he has helped fuel hatred that has driven Jihadists to commit terrorist acts over the past several years.

As an Islamic scholar, he has also been able to highlight anti-Semitic passages in the Qur'an and the hadiths, thereby lending the authority of the Prophet and Allah himself to the rising hatred of Jews. In another article he wrote:

"... Allah decreed that the Jews would be humiliated; he cursed them, and turned them into apes and pigs. Every time they ignite the fire of war, Allah extinguishes it. They disseminate corruption over the face of the earth, and fight the believers [Muslims] only from fortified villages or from behind walls ...

The political situation in the Middle East stands at stage center in the minds and hearts of millions of Muslims. Indeed, animosity toward Jews and Christians, toward Israel and the United States has permeated every segment of society and poisoned the thinking of professional men as well as the clergy and the media. For example, Dr. ʿAdel Sadeq, chairman of the Arab Psychiatrists Association and head of the department of psychiatry at ʿEin Shams University in Cairo, published an open letter to President Bush in an Egyptian newspaper that, to say the least, was less than scientific in tone and content.

He begins by telling the President that he is stupid.

Although you invest a lot of effort in proving yourself, you are not successful in doing so because you are stupid and understand nothing about what is happening in the world. "Stupidity" and "idiocy" are synonyms, and if you don't like the word "stupid," you are an evil person with an ugly soul.[54]

He claims he knew the President was stupid long before the rest of the world and explains how. But how?

Your stupidity is reflected in your facial features. Your face reminds me of the face of those who frequent a clinic for the mentally retarded. Your gaze is mindless and unfocused. Your eyes are misleading. Your facial expressions are incompatible with the matter [being discussed], and your tone of voice is completely disconnected from the content of your words—a salient characteristic of the mentally retarded.

I do not want to exaggerate by saying that your case is similar to cases I see at the clinic for the mentally retarded ...According to my personal judgment, and based on my 35 years of experience as a psychiatrist, your IQ is 110, and I challenge anyone who thinks otherwise.[55]

At this point, Dr. Sadeq, begins to lecture President Bush about foreign affairs and the troubling situation in the Middle East. Apparently as the result of his stupidity, the President is incapable of anti-Semitism. Sadeq enlightens him, speaking in language a sensitive therapist would hardly use with a mentally impaired patient.

Don't you understand, stupid, that Israel does not want peace? Don't you understand, stupid, that Sharon is a criminal murderer? Don't you understand, stupid, that the interests of your country are in great danger because of your complete bias in favor of Israel? Don't you understand, stupid, that the entire world is now standing against you and the policy of your administration? Don't you understand, stupid, that anyone who dies for the liberation of his homeland is a martyr? Don't you understand, stupid, that when a girl of 18 springs blows herself up, this means that her cause is right, and that her people will be victorious sooner or later?

I don't imagine, stupid, that you understand anything from my article, as your advisors hide things and thoughts of this kind from you so you will go on thinking you are smart. This means that class isn't over yet, you stupid idiot, you basest man in the world.[56]

Given Dr. Sadeq's position in the Arab professional world, one would expect a language more moderate, a case more carefully argued. His shrill tone, his absurd generalizations and bald-faced non sequiturs cast serious doubts on his own intellect and credibility. He sounds more like the patient than the doctor.

In this case, it is instructive to see how raging ideology, like a high fever, can destroy the ability of the mind to think clearly and to make those rational distinctions necessary for engaging in civilized discourse.

In addition to Dr. Al-Shwey'ir and Dr. Sadeq, Sheikh Muhammad Al-Gamei'a—the Al-Azhar University Representative in the United States and Imam of the Islamic Cultural Center and Mosque of New York City—has also allowed ideology to affect his thinking. While being interviewed on an Islamic website less than a month after September 11, he launched into a fanatic denunciation of Americans in general and Jewish Americans in particular.

After admitting that Muslims were treated well prior to the attacks on the World Trade Center and Pentagon, the sheikh charged that post-September 11, Muslims were the victims of widespread discrimination:

> Following the incident, Muslims and Arabs stopped feeling that it was safe to leave [their homes].... They stopped feeling that it was safe to send their wives to the market or their children to the schools. Muslims do not feel safe even going to the hospitals, because some Jewish doctors in one of the hospitals poisoned sick Muslim children, who then died.

Caught up in his own rhetoric, the sheikh began to propound a theory—common among Muslim activists—that it was the Jews who engineered the 9-11 attacks.

> During my conversations with this group [of anti-Muslim demonstrators], it became clear to me that they knew very well that the Jews were behind these ugly acts, while we, the Arabs, were innocent, and that someone from among their

people was disseminating corruption in the land. Although the Americans suspect that the Zionists are behind the act, none has the courage to talk about it in public.

Why are Americans afraid? The Sheikh knows what evil lurks in the hearts of Jews:

You know very well that the Zionists control everything and that they also control political decision-making, the big media organizations, and the financial and economic institutions. Anyone daring to say a word is considered an anti-Semite.

He even offers proof of this conspiracy:

All the signs indicate that the Jews have the most to gain from an explosion like that. They are the only ones capable of planning such acts. First of all, it was found that the automatic pilot was neutralized a few minutes before the flight, and the automatic pilot cannot be neutralized if you don't have command of the control tower. Second, the black boxes were found to contain no information; you cannot erase the information from these boxes if you do not plan it ahead of time on the plane. Third, America has the most powerful intelligence apparatuses, the FBI and the CIA ...How did the [perpetrators] manage to infiltrate America without their knowledge? Fourth, Jews control decision-making in the airports and in the sensitive centers in the White House and the Pentagon. Fifth, to date America has presented no proof incriminating Osama bin Laden and Al-Qua'ida....

...On the news in the U.S. it was said that four thousand Jews did not come to work at the World Trade Center on the day of the incident, and that the police arrested a group of Jews

rejoicing in the streets at the time of the incident.... This news
item was hushed up immediately after it was broadcast.... The
Jews who control the media acted to hush it up so that the American people would not know. If it became known to the American people, they would have done to the Jews what Hitler did!

But the sheikh didn't stop with this conspiracy theory. In the
same interview, he also blamed the Jews for every social ill afflict-
ing society, from Old Testament times to the present. His source
for this malevolent scrap of rhetoric—Allah himself.

The Jewish element is as Allah described it when he said, "They
disseminate corruption in the land." We know that they have
always broken agreements, unjustly murdered the prophets,
and betrayed the faith. Can they be expected to live up to their
contracts with us? These people murdered the prophets; do you
think they will stop spilling our blood? No ... You see these people all the time, everywhere, disseminating corruption, heresy,
homosexuality, alcoholism, and drugs. {Because of them] there
are strip clubs, homosexuals, and lesbians everywhere. They do
this to impose their hegemony and colonialism on the world.

Again, Gamei'a is not the Muslim equivalent of a backwoods
preacher who, in his ignorance, misreads the Bible and predicts
that, because of its wicked ways, the world will come to an end
next Thursday. This sheikh is an elite leader of the Muslim community in America. He speaks for Islamic higher education as
well as for the upper classes of his native Saudi Arabia. Thus he
lends academic and social prestige to the widespread Islamic idea
that neither Arabs nor Muslims are responsible for 9-11.

Arab writers throughout the world have offered similar theories:

- Columnist Ahmad Al-Muslih, whose thoughts run along the same dank channels, said: "What happened is, in my opinion, the product of Jewish, Israeli, and American Zionism, and the act of the great Jewish Zionist mastermind that controls the world's economy, media, and politics."[61]

- Hayat Al-Hweiek 'Atiya, a Lebanese-Jordanian said, "Maybe some will think that I am hallucinating things when I speak of Jewish Zionist hands behind the terrible event that struck at the U.S."[62]

- Jordanian columnist Rakan Al-Majali: "...it is clear that Israel is the one to benefit greatly from the bloody, loathsome terror operation that occurred yesterday, and that it seeks to benefit still more from by accusing the Arabs and Muslims of perpetrating this loathsome attack ...Only Israel does not fear the discovery that the Jews are behind this operation, if indeed it was so; who in the U.S. or outside it would dare to accuse them, as every blow to them means talk of a new "Holocaust"? They, more than anyone, are capable of hiding a criminal act they perpetrate, and they can be certain that no one will ask them about what they do."[63]

- Jihad Jabara, a columnist from Jordan, came up with an original twist—the Jews were wagging the dog: "I personally eliminate the possibility that Arab and Islamic organizations stood behind these acts ...Why [couldn't it be] that Zionist organizations perpetrated it, so that Israel could destroy the Al-Aqsa Mosque while the world was preoccupied with what was happening in America ...?"[64]

Through all of these comments runs the same strain of wishful thinking: "Wouldn't it be wonderful if it was the Jews all along?"

Underlying such theories is the ever-present fear of Jewish clev-
erness, Jewish chutzpa, Jewish power.

But there are alternative scapegoats as well—everybody, anybody but Muslims.

- A theorist from Jordan suspects religious fanatics in the
  United States, with a little help from the Jews. The cult he
  conjures up, however, bears little or no resemblance to any
  identifiable group of American flakes: "I say that Israel ben-
  efits from the explosions....We all know that there are
  extreme religious groups in the US who believe that the coming of the Messiah is near, and who aspire to purify Americans of all their human crimes. Among them are those who
  believe in committing suicide in order to reach Paradise,
  through punishing the human race. Mass suicide of entire
  groups has already occurred. We do not know whether Jews
  as well, more precisely the Mossad, have not had a hand in
  what happened, out of evil and dangerous intentions."[65]

- Samir Atallah, writing in the London daily *Al-Sharq Al-Awe-
  sat,* said: "I have a sneaking suspicion that George W. Bush was
  involved in the operation of September 11, as was Colin
  Powell."[66]

- Syrian columnist Hassan M. Yussef went rummaging back
  through history to find his scapegoat: "There is a possibility
  that this was [an act] of ancient retribution ...The US declared
  war on Japan, and used the atomic bomb for the first time,
  against Hiroshima and Nagasaki. [The bomb] killed more
  than 221,983 Japanese and was the cause of the Japanese defeat
  and the end of the war in 1945. Has the tragedy of Hiroshima
  and Nagasaki been resurrected sixty years later?"[67]

Abdallah bin Matruk Al-Haddal, preacher from the Ministry of
Islamic Affairs in Saudi Arabia, paints a similar picture of Jews while
appearing on "The Opposite Direction," an Al-Jazeera talk show.
To him, the September 11 attack was a Zionist plot; and he won-
ders why Americans allow themselves to be forever manipulated by
the Jews.

> I don't believe that the attack on America was perpetrated by
> bin Laden or the Muslims. I think differently. I believe it was
> a scheme. What is happening now is a continuation of an
> ancient attack. It is a concentration of the Jewish deception
> and the Jewish-Zionist wickedness which infiltrates the U.S....I
> am surprised that the Christian U.S. allows the 'brothers of
> apes and pigs' [meaning the Jews] to corrupt it. [The Jews]
> have murdered the prophets and the messengers. [The Jews]
> are the most despicable people who walked the land and are
> the worms of the entire world. They are all evil. And why?
> Because they are deceiving and plotting aggressors ..."[68]

In a further attempt to drive a wedge between Christians and
Jews, he attributes to the Jews the old slander that Jesus was born
to a woman who had had sex with an unknown man or men prior
to her marriage to Joseph. And he reminds his audience that the
Qur'an affirms the virgin birth and honors Jesus as a great prophet.

> ...The Jews do not respect Jesus, the son of Mary. America
> should know who the Jews truly are. The Jews see Jesus as
> someone born from prostitution, while he is the noble prophet
> of Allah, and his mother, peace be upon her, is pure ...[69]

In his eyes, Usama bin Laden becomes an American hero as
well as an Islamic hero, because he fights the Jews, who represent

falsehood and oppression—of which the U.S. is likewise the victim.

> ...Jewish fingerprints have infiltrated the U.S. Jewish evil and deception are those who attacked the U.S. [On September 11th] Osama bin Laden fought against the opposing falsehood and oppression that is generated by the evil and deceptive Jewish-Zionism ...[70]

He also depicts the American people as dupes of the media, which are little more than Jewish-operated opinion mills. Jews are arch-deceivers. Christians fare little better, since they are so gullible the Jews deceive them even about Christianity itself.

> ...The American people is a people that is being led by the media and TV culture. If a wicked Jewish crook begins saying that the Muslims are oppressors, it has an influence on the Americans. The media in America is in the hands of the Jews and behind it there are the Jewish Zionists' despicable fingerprints that change reality. They have even deceived the Christians about their own religion. Did you know that the person who forged the Christian religion is a Jew?[71]

Syria likewise produces its own brand of anti-Christian and anti-Semitic literature. Below are excerpts from "Shylock of New York and the Industry of Death," by Jbara Al-Barghuthi, writing in *Al-Usbu' Al-Adabi*, a Syrian publication.

These passages are particularly interesting because they include both an attack on the Jews (reviving the old lie that Jews use the blood of their enemies to make bread at Passover), and also an attack on Christian groups in the U.S. that openly support the State of Israel.

The Talmud's instructions, soaked in hatred and hostility toward humanity, are [stamped] in the Jewish soul. Throughout history, the world has known more than one Shylock. [The world has also known] more than one Toma as a victim of these Talmudic instructions and this hatred. [Toma was a Priest the Jews allegedly murdered in 1840, along with his Muslim servant, in order to use his blood in baking unleavened bread, Matzoh, for Passover.

Now Shylock of New York's time has arrived. He does not conceal his real intentions and is not ashamed of his evil deeds and his sins against humanity. Shylock of New York draws the elixir of his hatred and evil from all the extremism and fundamentalism on Earth. There are religious groups in the USA that are so fanatic for the Jews that they contradict their own Christian faith and support Israeli injustice toward Christian Arabs. They claim that an American who does not support Israel violates the will of God, for God has chosen the Jews and the men of the white flesh to be masters of humanity.[72]

Finally, to put these anti-Jewish attacks in perspective, consider a commentary on the history and character of Jews by the Palestinian Islamic Jihad weekly, *Al-Istiglal:*

The nature of the Jews is reflected in their hostile behavior. They were made of treachery and deceit and were marked by perfidy and treason. They rebelled [against God's orders] in evil and fornication and often unjustly killed prophets [who were sent to them.] They stole people's fortunes in false [claims.] Their love of life and of money pushed them to collect illegal usury. They were, also, in a constant state of conflict and continuous aggression driven by the evil rooted in the depths of their souls and their pressing desire to accumulate money in order to satisfy their unrestrained passions toward evil and in order to satiate their inclination to destruction.[73]

One would be hard-pressed to find a sin that didn't fall under one of the categories catalogued in this single paragraph. However, a common thread that runs throughout is the description of Jews as greedy, money mad, and unprincipled in business dealings.

There is little that is imaginative in these incessant Muslim attacks on Jews. They are like cheers at a football game—always the same, yet always delivered with fresh vigor. And they are designed to serve the same goal: to inspire the team to victory. By a constant barrage of bitter invective, militant Muslims intend to generate new acts of violence; another teenager wearing a belt of dynamite, another mass murder of Jews and Americans.

War fever is usually fueled by one or both of two passions: love of country and hatred of the enemy. The militant Muslim war on Jews and Christians is driven by something more—by a heightened religious fervor that transcends nationality and justifies unbridled hatred. Allah has blessed Islam and cursed Judaism. It is for Allah that Muslims fight and die. And it is Allah who speaks through the sheikhs and mullahs and academics to slander Jews wherever they may live, whatever their involvement—or lack of it—in the Middle East conflict.

Undoubtedly this explosion of anti-Semitic rhetoric has contributed immeasurably to the violence that has erupted over the past few years. Instead of reacting with uniform revulsion in the face of such malevolence, much of the world has grown silent and equivocal. In the United States, a surprising number of politicians, academics, and media commentators have sympathized with Islam and blamed Jews and Americans for the violence, both in the Middle East and in this country.

Meanwhile, political leaders who know better pretend that the attacks are the work of a few radical Muslim renegades who fail to understand their own faith. As this compilation of quotes should suggest, this is far from the truth.

CHAPTER SIX

Islam, Hitler, and the Holocaust

In the anti-Jewish diatribes of militant Islam, a disturbing and recurrent theme keeps popping up: an open admiration for Hitler, his Ultimate Solution, the Nazis, and the Holocaust. In the West, such sentiments provoke anger and contempt. In fact, to express revulsion at what the Nazis did to Jews during World War II, several Western nations (e.g., Germany, France, Canada) have outlawed anti-Semitic statements and denial of the Holocaust.

In the Middle East, however, militant Muslims don't deny or downplay the Holocaust; they celebrate it, openly expressing their admiration for Hitler and lamenting the fact that he did not succeed in his drive to eliminate the Jews from the face of the earth.

As an indication of how firmly anti-Semitism has taken root in some Muslim countries, the government of Iran recently republished the infamous *Protocols of the Elders of Zion*. This anti-Semitic tract—with murky origins in the nineteenth century—was allegedly a "handbook" for Jews to use in overthrowing and destroying all non-Jewish civilization. Its open declaration of malevolence reminds the sophisticated reader of a nineteenth-century melodrama, with Christian civilization tied to the railroad tracks and the stereotypical Jewish villain twisting his mustache and laughing up his sleeve. No serious scholar could believe it authentic. No decent person could support its publication and distribution.

Hitler, however, took the Protocols seriously enough to commend the book in *Mein Kampf*.

> ...To what extent the whole existence of this people is based on a continuous lie is shown incomparably by the *Protocols of the Wise Men of Zion*, so infinitely hated by the Jews. They are based on a forgery, the *Frankfurter Zeitung* moans and screams once every week: the best proof that they are authentic. What many Jews may do unconsciously is here consciously exposed. And that is what matters. It is completely indifferent from what Jewish brain these disclosures originate; the important thing is that with positively terrifying certainty they reveal the nature and activity of the Jewish people and expose their inner contexts as well as their ultimate final aims. The best criticism applied to them, however, is reality. Anyone who examines the historical development of the last hundred years from the standpoint of this book will at once understand the screaming of the Jewish press. For once this book has become the common property of a people, the Jewish menace may be considered as broken.[74]

Apparently the Iranian government took Hitler at his word and republished the Protocols. And, like the Führer, they had some comments to make on the text, lest an Iranian readership fail to understand fully the implications of the book. Consider the following excerpts from the official Iranian introduction:

The anti-human crimes, aggressions and murders committed by the Zionists and their inveterate rancor against Islam and Muslims are known to one and all ...

A boundless passion for usurpation and hegemony is typical of these professional criminals of history; a passion which they try to satisfy through their fickle logic of "From the Nile to the Euphrates."

For the last 35 years, in conspiration [*sic*] with the equally murderous superpowers, they have been getting closer and closer to their devilish objective.

... Not only has the complicity of the superpowers strengthened this cancerous tumor in the heart of the Islamic Middle-East, but also the silence of the Muslim Arab nations and the reactionary rulers of the region, has encouraged its aggressions and increased penetration.[75]

Iran is not the only nation to find in Hitler a paradigm for Muslims to emulate. By 1999 an Arabic version of *Mein Kampf* was being circulated in East Jerusalem and had risen to number 6 on the Palestinian best-seller list. In the "Introduction" to this paperback edition, translator Luis Al-Haj is full of grandiloquent praise for the late Führer:

Adolph Hitler was not an ordinary man to be [forgotten] by the wheels of time ...Adolph Hitler does not belong to the German people alone. He is one of the few great men who almost stopped the motion of history, altered its course, and changed the face of the world. Hence, he belongs to history.

...Hitler was a man of ideology who bequeathed an ideological heritage whose decay is inconceivable. This ideological heritage includes politics, society, science, culture, and war as science and culture.

The National Socialism that Hitler preached for and whose characteristics were presented in his book *My Struggle,* and whose principles he explained in his speeches before he took power, as well as during the 13 years he spent as head of the German nation—this National Socialism did not die with the death of its herald, Rather, its seeds multiplied under each star.

...We cannot really understand the efforts of this man without examining the principles enclosed in his book *My Struggle* that the Nazis turned into the "Gospel of National Socialism."

This translation of the book *My Struggle* has never been presented to Arab speakers. It is taken from the original text of the author, Adolph Hitler. The text was untouched by the censor. We made a point to deliver Hitler's opinions and theories on nationalism, regimes, and ethnicity without any changes because they are not yet outmoded and because we, in the Arab world, still proceed haphazardly in all three fields.[76]

Paradoxically, though Middle Eastern Muslims sometimes compare the United States to Nazi Germany in its drive for world domination, many of their sermons and commentaries commend Hitler for his attempt to rid the world of the Jewish menace. Ahmad Ragab, a commentator whose column also appears in *Al-Akhbar,* published a two-sentence tribute to Hitler that would have embarrassed racist David Duke.

Thanks to Hitler of blessed memory, who on behalf of the Palestinians, revenged in advance, against the most vile criminals on the face of the earth. Although we do have a complaint against him for his revenge on them was not enough.[77]

Apparently the column drew praise from his Egyptian readers, because in the following weeks, he ran the same two-sentence statement again and again.

The thesis here is particularly ironic because it praises Hitler for actions that ultimately led to the founding of the State of Israel. Had the Nazi government not persecuted the Jews—had not the Holocaust occurred—there would have been no hoards of homeless Jews after World War II, displaced persons who had no reason or desire to return to Germany, Austria, Poland, or to any other part of Europe that had fallen under Hitler's domination.

Given Ragab's attitude towards the Middle Eastern situation, he might better have cursed Hitler, not thanked him, for the atrocities of the 1930s and 1940s.

Consider, also, this selection from a column written by Anis Mansour and published in the government-sponsored Egyptian newspaper, *Al-Ahram*. It is among the most contrived of all Holocaust justifications.

> [Without Israeli casualties,] it would become clear to the world that what happened to the Jews of Germany, Poland, and Russia, was justified. It is not true that all the Jews are peaceniks. There is a suicidal sect among them that does not desire to live. [Therefore,] they kindle the people's hatred and hostility and, as a result, people turn against them. Although there are many intelligent people among them, they use their intellect to devise new ways for people everywhere to hate them and unite against them.
>
> There are sects in Israel that view the Jewish state as a heretic state. They believe the Israelites deserve to be tortured and that what Hitler did to the Jews of the West is an appropriate punishment for their mistreatment of the Jews of the East....[78]

In the other words, not only did the Jews bring the Holocaust on themselves, but they did so deliberately—making themselves as odious as possible in order to incur the righteous wrath of non-Jews. According to Mansour, these deliberately obnoxious Jews are possessed by a death wish that makes them seek their own destruction as a people. His account of the formation of Israel, however, suggests that the Jews want to survive after all—and do so by hiding behind the United States and European nations.[79]

Al-Akhbar, the Egyptian government daily, published an article by Fatma Abdallah Mahmoud that was nothing more than wild-eyed invective against all Jews, past and present. There is little concrete detail to hold this stream of insults together. Like so many others, Mahmoud commends Hitler for his intentions, but laments his ultimate lack of success in eliminating the Jews from the face of the earth. All in all, it is a diatribe the likes of which would never have appeared in a respectable U.S. newspaper, even if directed against the Japanese or Germans at the height of World War II.

Here are a few excerpts:.

> They are accursed in heaven and on earth. They are accursed from the day the human race was created and from the day their mothers bore them. They are accursed also because they murdered the Prophets. They murdered the Prophet John the Baptist and served up his head on a golden platter to the singer and dancer Salome. Allah also cursed them with a thousand curses when they argued with and resisted his words of truth, deceived the Prophet Moses, and worshiped the golden calf that they created with their own hands!![80]

He accuses the Jews of inventing the Holocaust, which he terms a "fraud." He speaks of studies that prove the concentration camps were fiction, but he never cites the specific works. His readers are expected to accept these generalizations on his authority.

Many French studies have proven that this is no more than a fabrication, a lie, and a fraud!! That is, it is a "scenario" the plot of which was carefully tailored, using several faked photos completely unconnected to the truth. Yes, it is a film, no more and no less. Hitler himself, whom they accuse of Nazism, is in my eyes no more than a modest "pupil" in the world of murder and bloodshed. He is completely innocent of the charges of frying them in the hell of his false Holocaust!!

The entire matter, as many French and British scientists and researchers have proven, is nothing more than a huge Israeli plot aimed at extorting the German government in particular and the European countries in general. But I, personally and in light of this imaginary tale, complain to Hitler, even saying to him from the bottom of my heart, "If only you had done it, brother, if only it had really happened, so that the world could sigh in relief [without] their evil and sin."

They always try to warp and distort everything fair and beautiful!! Basically, they are a model of moral ugliness, debasement, and degradation. If only Allah would curse them more and more, to the end of all generations. Amen.[81]

Holocaust denial is illegal in Canada, as it is in some European nations. Several years ago, following the Canadian trial of a Holocaust denier,—an article on the trial appeared in the Palestinian newspaper *Al-Manar,* insisting that the systematic murder of millions of Jews was a fabrication invented by the Jews themselves.

Nobody in the West dares to stand up, when the subject is the fictitious Nazi Holocaust against the Jews of Europe. Since the end of World War II, the victors have imposed their hegemony over history, and forged the legend of the Holocaust to extort the entire world, using the face of the ugly Nazi. They planted a thorn in the side of defeated Germany to extort it forever.[82]

It is by no means surprising that many Middle Eastern Muslims find Hitler's ideas attractive. The similarities between Hitler's vision and that of some Muslim leaders, like the Ayatollah Khomeini, are are both startling and striking.

- Both believe in government by a strong, charismatic leader.
- Both regimes have religious overtones—Hitler's, to be sure, more "quasi-religious" than Islamic theocracy. (Al-Haj alludes to this quality in Nazism by calling *Mein Kampf* the "Gospel of National Socialism.")
- Both are dedicated to world conquest in the name of their vision of what society should be.
- Both are willing, indeed eager, to engage and kill enemies on the field of battle in order to achieve their goals.
- Both are passionately anti-Jewish and assign a high priority to the killing of Jews—their ultimate enemies.
- At heart, both display a kind of primitive power that moves the masses with highly charged rhetoric and appeals to a mythic past and an apocalyptic future.

The most charitable way to explain this pro-Nazi rhetoric is to attribute it to Middle Eastern ignorance—Hitler would *not* have considered the Arabs "Aryan," any more than the Jews. In addition, to say that militant Muslims fail to understand the impact the Third Reich made on Western historical consciousness. Both liberals and conservatives in Europe and the Americas regard Hitler as a monster, a madman driven by hatred and

ideology. Thus Westerners are uniformly horrified by these statements which sound, at best, like adolescent bravado, at worst like
expressions of contempt for humanity itself.

Is this militant rhetoric, then, the product of ignorance? Or
do those who express the most admiration for Hitler understand
fully the implications of what they are saying and saying it any-
way? In either case, it is difficult to excuse such incendiary remarks
or to see them as anything less than the purest kind of malice.

CHAPTER SEVEN

Islamic Prejudice Against Christians

When Muslims and their apologists extol Islam's respect
for and tolerance of Christians, they usually offer as
Exhibit A the Prophet Muhammad's 628 Charter of Privileges to
Christians, enunciated in a letter to the monks at St. Catherine's
Monastery on Mount Sinai. Muslim advocates Zahoor and Haq
offer the following English translation:

> This is a message from Muhammad ibn Abdullah, as a covenant
> to those who adopt Christianity, near and far, we are with them.
>
> Verily I, the servants, the helpers, and my followers defend
> them, because Christians are my citizens; and by Allah! I hold
> out against anything that displeases them.
>
> No compulsion is to be on them.
>
> Neither are their judges to be removed from their jobs nor
> their monks from their monasteries.

No one is to destroy a house of their religion, to damage it, or to carry anything from it to the Muslims' houses.

Should anyone take any of these, he would spoil God's covenant and disobey His Prophet. Verily, they are my allies and have my secure charter against all that they hate.

No one is to force them to travel or to oblige them to fight. The Muslims are to fight for them.

If a female Christian is married to a Muslim, it is not to take place without her approval. She is not to be prevented from visiting her church to pray.

Their churches are to be respected. They are neither to be prevented from repairing them nor the sacredness of their covenants.

No one of the nation (Muslims) is to disobey the covenant till the Last Day (end of the world).[83]

This document seems to be the epitome of religious tolerance, particularly since it was written in an age when theological differences were often settled by disembowelment. If all succeeding generations of Muslims had followed this document in spirit as well as in letter, the map of the modern world might be very different.

The Christian population at that time was less combative, less likely to subvert or overthrow his theocracy. The promises made to the monks were undoubtedly reassuring to Christians—as long as they didn't read between the lines. What he left unsaid, what he said elsewhere and what he and his followers did painted a more disturbing picture.

For example, the Christian bride could continue to follow her faith, what if her husband chose to convert to Christianity? Muhammad proclaimed that death was an appropriate penalty for "the one who turns renegade from Islam and leaves the group of Muslims." In other words, if a Muslim converts to Christianity, he deserves the death penalty. *The Reliance of the Traveller*, a Sunni collection of hadiths, says the same thing: "[W]hen a person who has reached puberty and is sane voluntarily apostatizes from Islam, he deserves to be killed."[84]

The same scripture also restricts where Christians may live. They were "forbidden to reside in the Hijaz, meaning the area and towns around Mecca, Medina, and Yamama, for more than three days."[85]

The ancient Islamic policy was set down by one of Muhammad's close companions—Umar, the second caliph (634–644), who cited Muhammad himself as his authority. An early successor to the Prophet, Umar reflects the limits of Muslim tolerance of Christianity, despite what Muhammad the diplomat may have said.[86]

The same hostility prevails among many Muslims today. Consider first the statement of Usama bin Laden following an attack on a U.S. military installation in Saudi Arabia, where bin Laden was born and grew up. Nineteen people were killed.

This statement—"Declaration of War Against the Americans Occupying the Land of the Two Holy Places" [Saudi Arabia]—is subtitled "Expel the Polytheists from the Arabian Peninsula" and is a diatribe filled with quasi-theological references to "Zionist-Crusader atrocities against Muslims worldwide, and the promise of Islamic terrorism as Allah's retribution. He laments the "occupation" of Saudi-Arabia by the American enemy, and warns his Muslim brothers:

> The money you pay to buy American goods will be transformed into bullets and used against our brothers in Palestine and tomorrow (future) against our sons in the land of the two Holy places. By buying these goods we are strengthening their economy while our dispossession and poverty increases.[87]

Addressing the U.S. Secretary of Defense, he boasts of the willingness of Muslim youth to die in Jihad for their faith.

These youths love death as you love life. They inherit dignity, pride, courage, generosity, truthfulness and sacrifice from father to father. They are most delivering and steadfast at war.[88]

At the same time, he reminds Muslims of Allah's promise of paradise for all who die in Jihad, as revealed in scripture:

"A martyr's privileges are guaranteed by Allah; forgiveness with the first gush of his blood, he will be shown his seat in paradise, he will be decorated with the jewels of belief (Imaan), married off to the beautiful ones, protected from the test of the grave, assured security in the day of judgment, crowned with the crown of dignity, a ruby of which is better than this whole world (Duniah) and its entire content, wedded to seventy-two of the pure Houris (beautiful ones of Paradise) and his intercession on the behalf of seventy of his relatives will be accepted" (narrated by Ahmad and Al-Tirmithi, with the correct and trustworthy reference).

Those youths know that their rewards in fighting you, the USA, is double than their rewards in fighting someone else not from the people of the book. They have no intention except to enter paradise by killing you. An infidel, and enemy of God like you, cannot be in the same hell with his righteous executioner.[89]

Bin Laden would undoubtedly view with contempt the definitions of Jihad by "moderate" Muslim groups. For him, the word is synonymous with warfare against Christians ("Crusaders," who worship three gods), as well as against Jews.

As Muslims—legal and illegal—pour into the United States to find employment, the followers of Usama bin Laden and those who believe in violent Jihad seek to expel all foreign workers from Muslim countries in the Middle East. It is important to understand precisely why: It is not because the workers are from America or Europe or, for that matter, some other Middle Eastern nation. It is for religious reasons. One Muslim website explains the situation as follows:

> No doubt the Prophet ...ordered for the expulsion of the polytheists from the Arabian peninsula. He said:"((I will surely expel the Jews and the Christians from the Arabian Peninsula so that I leave (there) none but Muslims."))) The hadeeth indicates that the Guidance of the Prophet ...is that the Arabian Peninsula should remain with only Muslim inhabitants, due to the danger posed by the presence of Christians and other disbelievers.[90]

Some of the more militant Jihadists believe that Saudi Arabia is no longer a Muslim country because it allows American technicians and military personnel—i.e., Christians—to work there. An article called "Saudi Arabia is not an Islamic State," quotes Allah himself on the subject:

> And Allah says: "Oh you who believe! Do not take the Jews and Christians as friends and protectors. They are but friends and protectors to each other, and whoever amongst you turns to them [for friendship], then surely he is one of them. Verily, Allah does not guide an unjust people."[91]

Sheikh Ibn Baz refers to this hadith in his Al Fatawi, volume 1, page 202 (1988). In this decree, he prohibits the hiring of non-Muslims even as servants, decrying the fact that in Saudi Arabia "at least 5,000 non-Muslim U.S. military personnel to be stationed in Saudi Arabia, as well as a large number of foreign, non-Muslim scientific, technical and managerial workers in the petrochemical industry."

At first glance, one might conclude that these are merely a few dissidents complaining about the tolerance of the Saudi Arabian government. However, don't be fooled into believing that the nation is tolerant of Christians, despite the fact that the U.S. government and the American media often refer to Saudi Arabia as a "friendly" Arab nation. They say little about the official mistreatment of Christians in that country—perhaps because the Saudis supply the West with oil and perhaps because the United States has some strategic use for the country. In fact, many prominent Saudis are aggressive and unapologetic in their persecution of Christians, whether Arabs or Westerners.

For example, it is illegal for Christians and other non-Muslims to congregate to worship. In fact, it is against the law to build a Christian church in Saudi Arabia. Also, Christians and other non-Muslims are forbidden to wear crosses or any other symbols of their faith, which means they can't carry Bibles in public. Some travelers have had their Bibles confiscated by customs and tossed into paper shredders. All this, despite the fact that Christians make up approximately four percent of the population.

Here are some examples of how Islamic law is put into practice in Saudi Arabia. To Americans, they seem as repressive as the laws of totalitarian regimes in twentieth-century Europe. To Saudis, they merely reflect the culture of the nation—ancient, traditional, immutable. International Christian Concern, a U.S. watchdog organization, has the recorded the following:

• Despite the fact that the Saudi government states officially that it permits non-Muslims to worship in the privacy of their own homes, a Christian worker was arrested near Jeddah and interrogated about meetings that he and his wife held in their home. The Mutawa'ah—the religious police—invaded his house and confiscated his computer, photo albums, Bibles, song books, and his audio cassettes and video-tapes. Among other things, they were looking for the names of others who also worshipped in homes.[92]

- A man was hauled from his home, thrown in jail and charged with conducting a small Bible study in his house. Muslim co-workers had turned him in to the Mutawa'ah.[93]

- On January 7, 2000, police burst into a Christian gathering of around 100 people and arrested fifteen of the group—five of them children. Christians concluded that the police took the children in order to force their parents to reveal the names and activities of other Christians. All fifteen were eventually deported.[94]

- Two Christians were arrested and sentenced to 150 lashes—a frequent punishment for "religious deviation" in Saudi Arabia. Their employer was told they would be deported after thirty days. Had they been converts from Islam, they would have been subject to hanging under the strict rules of Shari'a.[95]

- Authorities beat and kicked three Ethiopian Christians, then suspended them with chains and gave each 80 lashes with a flexible metal cable. They had been arrested after a citizen complained about foreign Christians renting a public hall for a farewell party. The three smuggled a letter to the outside which, among other things, reported: "Our bodies are wounded, swollen, terribly bruised, and with great pain …Baharu's kidney may have been damaged and he is passing blood with his urine. When we reported to the prison hospital for treatment, we were slapped and told to come back after we were dead. It seems as if we were brought [here] to be tortured and tormented to death."[96]

Watani, a Coptic weekly published in Egypt, reported that Arab Christians were emigrating from Saudi Arabia in large numbers and cited numerous examples of harassment to suggest why they were leaving. None of these incidents is life threatening, but they illustrate the deep-seated hostility toward Christians and Christianity that is part of the culture of the country. Here are but three.

- A Greek in Saudi Arabia on business was hassled at the airport in Jeddah by customs officials who ripped a cross from his neck and threw it into the waste basket.[97]
- A European woman, the wife of a Muslim, had in her luggage an icon of the Virgin Mary which her grandmother had given her. Customs searched her luggage, found the icon, and confiscated it.[98]
- A Christian walking in downtown Jeddah was accosted by the Mutawa'ah. One of the officers asked the man why he wasn't in the mosque at that very moment, praying to Allah. When the man said he was a Christian, the policeman cried out in anger and spat in the man's face.[99]

Curiously, the U.S. Department of State has even allowed the Mutawa'ah to cast their shadow over religious conduct within the walls of the American Embassy in Saudi Arabia. While stationed there, Timothy Hunter, a Roman Catholic, was allowed to attend Mass every Sunday inside the Embassy. Other denominations, however, were forbidden to hold religious services, even though, under international law, the American Embassy sits on sovereign U.S. soil. When Hunter protested the treatment of the other Christians, the Embassy canceled the Mass.[100]

It is difficult for Americans to understand a nation that practices religious repression so unapologetically. In our own country, Muslims are guaranteed the same constitutional protections as Christians, which means they can do whatever Muslims do in mosques without fear of government interference. So why this difference in attitude and policy?

One factor is the First Amendment to the U.S. Constitution, which guarantees religious freedom. But other Western nations allow Muslims and Buddhists and Hindus to worship as they please—and without the First Amendment to guide them. The Saudis and militant Islamic nations hold a different view of Islam.

Far from believing in the separation of religion and government, these Muslims see the chief mission of the state as the imposition of Shari'a on their own people, and eventually on the rest of the world.

Rather than entertain doubts about forcing their beliefs on others—doubts that would arise immediately in the consciences of most Americans—Saudi Muslims believe in religious absolutism. If the Prophet Muhammad derived his vision from Allah, then Islam (which means "submission") is the only religion for the world—and the sooner Christians and other non-Muslims accept this truth, the sooner the earth's troubles will melt like lemon drops.

One of the things Saudis fear most is Christian proselytizing. They are well-aware that in southern Sudan, Muslims left Islam in huge numbers and converted to Christianity. Consequently, in obedience to Shari'a, the Sudanese government began slaughtering or starving Sudanese Christians by the hundreds of thousands. The Saudis have tried to prevent any Christian materials from penetrating their system which then requires censoring. And this policy even includes the Internet.

A study by Harvard's Berkman Center for Internet & Society reported that approximately 250 religious but non-Islamic websites are systematically blocked by the Saudi government's Internet Services Unit. These sites include Answering-Islam.org, ReligiousTolerance.org, sites for the Family Bible Hour and Arabic Bible Outreach, and websites for individual Christian congregations. Curiously, the Saudis also block Christian anti-porn sites, perhaps because they want their people to believe that Christians favor pornography.[101]

Yet in the United States, Saudis enjoy the right to worship as they please and even to use our media and educational system to promote Islam among American Christians.

Recently, PBS—which operates with federal funding—ran a two-part series on Islam that presented the Prophet and Muslims in the most flattering light imaginable. If it looked like an infomercial for Islam, that's because it was: The Kingdom of Saudi Arabia was one of its key sponsors, Saudi oil dollars commingling with U.S. tax dollars. No program that presented Christianity in such a favorable light would ever appear on Saudi TV (or, for that matter, on PBS).

In Northern Virginia, the Kingdom of Saudi Arabia also operates the Islamic Saudi Academy, whose stated purpose is "to study Islam and the Arabic language ...in an atmosphere conducive to building Muslim character." No Christian academies are allowed in Saudi Arabia.

CHAPTER EIGHT

The Killing of Christians

To see how much further Muslims can go in their enforcement of Shari'a, consider what has happened to Christians in Sudan, Africa's largest country. Sudan is about one-third the size of the United States and has a population of approximately 34 million. Yet over the past nineteen years, 1.9 million people—about one out of every seventeen citizens—has died in a bloody civil war that has strong anti-Christian origins. Nearly 300,000 southern Sudanese, mostly Christian, have left the country; and about 80 percent have been driven from their homes at least once.[102]

At the heart of this conflict is the desire of the Government of Sudan (GoS) to impose Islamic law on all the peoples of the nation—140 ethnic groups speaking approximately 117 dialects.[103] The population in the northern region tends to be Muslim, while the population in the south is predominantly tends to be Christian.

In 1960 the Christians in southern Sudan numbered about five percent of the region's population. Forty-two years later, that proportion had increased to 70 percent.[104] Since militant Islam cannot allow the growth of any other religion within its sphere of influence, General Hassan Omer al-Bashir, President of Sudan, declared Jihad against the people of the south.

Over the years, GoS has killed or scattered hundreds of thousands of southern Sudanese Christians. The government has bombed the civilian population, killing many. In 1999 there were 65 confirmed bombings of civilians. In 2000, there were 132. And in 2001, there were 195.[105]

Most Christians, however, have died of starvation. The Institute on Religion and Democracy, a watchdog organization, has this to say of GoS: "...their most potent weapon of all is the capability and willingness to engineer famine. (In February 1998 up to 100,000 southern Sudanese died in a matter of weeks in a GoS-engineered famine)."[106]

In late September of 2002, GoS blocked humanitarian flights in and out of southern Sudan, already in shambles as the result of years of bombing. The Muslim government would not allow food and medical supplies to be brought in, and the wounded and ill could not be evacuated. This action meant the end of Operation Lifeline Sudan flights, which had been brought 150 tons of food to the southern Sudanese each day.[107]

In fact, USAID.com, a government website, reports the following:

> In addition to the direct threat to non-combatants from these aerial bombings, there are additional humanitarian issues associated with the Government's tactic of bombarding civilian and humanitarian targets. There is a direct relationship between GOS aerial bombardment and GOS flight denials of U.N. Operation Lifeline Sudan (OLS) humanitarian operations and evacuating staff. Furthermore, GOS aerial bombardments raise significant security concerns with OLS officials that often lead to the U.N. suspending operations to an insecure area. In addition, the abduction of humanitarian staff and killing of relief workers has a direct relationship to the GOS bombardment of civilian and humanitarian targets because GOS bombardment appears to be part of an overall government policy on restricting humanitarian access.[108]

By September of 2002, the GoS had launched dozens of air and ground attacks killing hundreds of southern Sudanese and

displacing tens of thousands more. Africa Christian Faith in Action
reported from Khartoum:

- GOS bombers and hundreds of holy warriors [jihadists] were
  flown out of the capital daily, on their way to the predominantly Christian south;
- The roads were jammed with military trucks, equipment,
  and troops, also headed south;
- Southerners in Khartoum were increasingly subject to arrests
  and beatings—some simply disappeared;
- A Dinka evangelical churchman was beaten so badly that he
  died;
- Throughout Khartoum, the government was whipping up
  sentiment for Jihad—on the radio and TV, in the newspa-
  pers, and on the streets with loudspeakers.[109]

At the close of 2001, GoS/Muslim forces alternately offered
assurances of peace and then attacked Christians in the south.
Here are selections from a USAID report documenting the atrocities as 2002 drew to a close:

- On October 5, 7, and 8, GoS planes bombed the village of
  Mangayat. The bombing coincided with airdrops of food to
  twenty thousand displaced persons—despite the fact that
  GoS had cleared the humanitarian efforts.
- On November 2, GoS forces and Mujahadeen militia attacked
  Nyamliel.
- Despite U.S. attempts to negotiate a peace agreement during
  the months of November, December, and January, the U.N.
  reported the GoS bombing of two villages on January 11.
- On February 10 a GoS plane dropped six bombs, killing two
  people. Again, the attack coincided with the distribution of
  food to more than 18,000 starving people.

- On February 15, GoS bombs killed a Sudanese health worker and four civilians.
- On February 20, a GoS military helicopter fired several rockets into a WFP food distribution center in the village of Bieh, killing 24 people and wounding many others. Again, the time had been cleared by GoS, so the government knew precisely when the distribution would take place.
- GoS denied access by humanitarian care-givers to more than 45 locations on the March OLS flight schedule and also to 18 new locations. The U.N. reported that this blockage of humanitarian aid could affect more than 345,000 people in Southern Sudan—again, predominantly Christians.[110]

The pattern of the attacks here is unmistakable. The targets were not only southern Sudanese civilians—as opposed to rebel military units—but also humanitarian efforts to feed non-combatants and to administer medical care. The Islamic government has continued to attack Christians on the one hand, and to starve them to death on the other.

The World Evangelical Alliance issued a report in June of 2002 that documented additional atrocities:

The Southern Sudanese are suffering intensely. Slavery is endemic, aerial bombardment is routine, and the Government of Sudan (GoS) continues to orchestrate famine as a weapon of mass genocide. Though rich in resources, Sudan is reduced to poverty by the GoS spending about a million dollars a day on its jihad against the South. An international panel investigating slavery in Sudan recently reported that it was "commonplace," with Southern villagers being abducted during raids by pro-government militias. Victims are forced to convert to Islam. In the Western Upper Nile, some 32 people died and massive casualties were inflicted when a relief centre and four other villages were bombed on 22–26 May.[111]

The goal of General al-Bashir has been to kill Christians or to drive them out of the country. In fact, Bashir's treatment of Christians in southern Sudan parallels precisely Muhammad's treatment of Medina's Jews in the seventh century: some he has expelled, some he has killed, and some he has sold into slavery.

The current government of Iran, which was elected in 1997, has boasted of its restoration of religious rights to non-Muslims. However, Iranian Christians International—an organization based in Colorado Springs—reports that the treatment of Christians in Iran has actually worsened over the past five or six years. The Iranian religious police carry on their own harsh brand of anti-Christian persecution. In addition, the government has also allowed Muslim vigilantes to enforce Shari'a.

Abe Ghaffari, ICI executive director, says the government is also killing Christians: "We can confirm eight deaths since 1988 and between 15 and 22 disappearances in 1997 and 1998—one must presume that most or all were murdered—and 3 three disappearances in 2000."[112]

- The Rev. Mehdi Dibaj was imprisoned for nine years "because he refused to deny his faith in Christ." The 60-year-old Dibaj was released after an international campaign on his behalf but was murdered three months later.[113]
- The Rev. Mohammad Bagher Yusefi, pastor of the Assemblies of God, who cared for Dibaj's two sons during the nine years of imprisonment, was himself murdered. He left his home for prayer and was found dead, hanging from a tree.

Yusefi had been born a Muslim; and according to Shari'a, his punishment for conversion was death.[114]

- The Rev. Mr. Sayyah, a priest in Shiraz, had his throat cut, and the son of an Anglican bishop was shot. A church leader in Mashad was hanged in prison. Bishop Haik Hovsepian Mehr, chairman of the Protestant Council of Ministers was murdered. And so was his successor, the Rev. Tateos Michaelian.[115]

These attacks on Iranian Christians were brutal but conventional. However, Jeff M. Sellers, writing in *Christianity Today,* reported a government-engineered execution that was considerably more diabolic:

In the fall of 1997, authorities released several Iranian Christians whom they had injected with radioactive material. They apparently wanted the Christians to die but not on police premises, according to International Christian Concern. The radioactive material was detected when one of the men had an x-ray and received treatment. The other prisoners have since disappeared.[116]

While in Iran Christians tend to be murdered one at a time, in Nigeria, Muslim religious leaders prefer massacres. When a reporter wrote in a news article that, had he been alive, Muhammad would have married one of the contestants of the Miss World Pageant, Muslims took to the streets. First they burned and looted the newspaper office. Then they went after Christians. Bishop Josiah Fearon of Kaduna confirmed that the attacks were instigated by Muslim leaders and were motivated by religious zealotry.

"Our people had nothing whatsoever to do with either the article or this contest but we have been victimized by Muslim rioters for political ends." [117]

In the end, rioters killed over two hundred, injured more than twelve hundred, and drove some twelve thousand from their homes. At the height of the uprising, Muslim youths set up roadblocks and checked the religious beliefs of motorists, attacking the Christians they found.[118]

It is comforting to believe that the current struggle between Palestinians and Israelis has caused Middle Eastern Muslims to see only the belligerent side of the Prophet and the Qur'an, that theirs is a heresy brought about by circumstance. However, the Middle East is not the only region where Muslims believe that "Jihad" means fighting for Allah and the Prophet. Indonesia has produced its own Jihad, which has resulted in thousands of Christian deaths.

Since 1998 the Maluku Islands (also known as the Spice Islands) have been the scene of violent clashes between Muslims and Christians.

In August of 1999, East Timor, in a U.N. supervised election, voted for independence from Indonesia. Indonesia withdrew its occupation forces, but not before the militia loyal to the Jakarta government had driven three hundred thousand people from their homes and killed hundreds of Christians.[119]

In early 2000, the violence boiled over again when a false report reached Jakarta that two thousand Muslims had been massacred by Christians on Halmahera, a remote island in the Northern part of the Malukus. The government denied the report, but thousands of Muslims took to the streets in Jakarta, chanting "Jihad! Jihad!" against Christians. Wearing traditional Muslim garb, some five thousand stormed into the streets, slaughtered a goat, and smeared a cross with its blood.[120]

Later, Catholic World News reported that Christians in the Malukus were being forced to convert to Islam at gunpoint. A

Mosque spokesman admitted the conversions, but said: "The claim that they were forced to become Muslims is baseless. They voluntarily converted to Islam."[121]

Christians told a different tale. According to Associated Press Television, several males said that they had been forced to convert, to be circumcised, and to have their heads shaved.

"I only said yes to save myself," said Anton Sagat, one of dozens who escaped the island in a boat.

Another said, "A soldier aimed a pistol at our chests. He said if we refused to become Muslims we would be shot."

Speaking at a mosque, Indonesian President Abdurrahman—himself a moderate Muslim—admitted as much, saying, "There is an effort by Islamic extremists to convert Christians to Islam in the Malukus. This is not right."[122] Occasionally, moderate Muslims do decry the actions of the extremists.

And who is responsible for this Jihad? Most of the trouble has been perpetrated by the Indonesian Laskar Jihad, a guerrilla army led by Ja'far Umar Thalib, who claims a force of ten thousand. Indeed, what is happening in Indonesia is reminiscent of Communist strategy during the Cold War. Stir up trouble in a Third World country, foment street riots, recruit a guerrilla force, and begin a "war of liberation." Thalib is the Che Guevara of Indonesia, only his goal is the establishment not of a secular socialist regime but of a theocracy in which Muslims rule supreme.

Christians are a minority in Indonesia, which is the most populous Islamic nation in the world. It is small wonder that the radical Muslims, with their imperialist dreams, would attempt to destabilize the country and eventually kill, drive out, or convert the Christians among them.

The original cause of this ongoing carnage is in dispute. The initial violence occurred in the aftermath of a dispute between a

Christian bus driver and a would-be passenger who was Muslim.

Christianity Today offered the following explanation in August of 2000: "More recently, trained fighters of the 'Laskar Jihad' " (Banner of Holy War) have entered Ambon to eliminate the Christian population and establish a Muslim state on the island."[123]

The activities of the Laskar Jihad have proved devastating to Christians.

- In the summer of 2000, *Christianity Today* reported that in a period of only twenty months approximately 500,000 Christians were driven from their homes, 455 churches were destroyed, and the well-armed, well-trained 'jihad' warriors killed more than 2,500, publicly declaring they would "push all Christians off the island or kill them."[124]

- According to a reporter who was on the scene, the attack was well-planned. As *Christianity Today* summarizes it: "Navy gunboats lobbed shells onto the beach and sprayed cannon fire in the ocean, giving cover fire for craft carrying jihad fighters. Other forces, camped for days in the mountains behind, descended in a coordinated assault. Destruction was quick and thorough, the reporter said. The next night angry Christians retaliated by attacking a Muslim village on a neighboring island, burning homes."[125]

- In a radio address in May of 2002, Thalib exhorted Muslims to wage Jihad against the Christian community: "Prepare the bombs which we have. Prepare the ammunition which we are ready to vomit forth from the barrels of the weapons we possess. And we swear by Allah! By Allah! By Allah! Until Tentena and surroundings become a sea of fire."[126]

- Armed Muslims in Central Sulawesi began stopping cars and buses and checking religious IDs. As Mona Saroinsong,

Coordinator of the Crisis Centre of the General Synod of Protestant Churches in North and Central Sulawesi put it: "While the Christians check passing cars for weapons, the Muslims check for identity. And if they find a Christian, they will take him or her away. We fear that many have been killed in this way."[127]

- Soinsong also reported that five Christians had been killed while traveling on a bus, and a man on another bus had "disappeared without a trace."[128]

- Some Christians believe that elements in the military are sympathetic with the activities of Laskar Jihad and are collaborating with the terrorists. In the summer of 2002, the army withdrew protective troops from several villages in the Malukus; and shortly thereafter Muslims, dressed in black and wielding automatic weapons, arrived on the scene and burned the two villages to the ground, Sepe for the second time. The Reverend Vence Waani, pastor of the Sepe Pentecostal Church, described the scene as follows: "The sound of automatic weapons was coming from every direction mixed with the hysterical voices of mothers calling for their children, and shrieks of fear from the children. The flames were engulfing the houses. It was a scene of horror." The terrorists burned both towns to the ground. Among the casualties: Waani's newly built church, as well as another Protestant house of worship.

Organizations concerned with the welfare of Christians worldwide regard those killed in the Maluku islands as martyrs—men and women who died because they professed the faith. And there are thousands whose deaths will never be mourned by any nation, whose families will never be compensated for their loss.

In Pakistan, Ayub Masih, a Christian, was arrested and imprisoned on October 14, 1996, charged with blasphemy against the Prophet Muhammad. Neighbors accused him of uttering offensive remarks and telling them to read *The Satanic Verses,* a forbidden book in Islam. He was tried by the Sessions Court Sahiwal and sentenced to death.

In fact, Ayub Masih's neighbor, Sharif Muhammad Akram, fabricated the blasphemy charge to acquire property that belonged to the defendant's family. After a six-year appeals process, the three-panel Supreme Court finally ruled that the defendant was innocent and released him.

However, six other Christians are still being held on blasphemy charges,; and two have already been sentenced to death. According to International Christian Concern: "Blasphemy prisoners are often beaten by other inmates, and may be denied a blanket, food or medicine."

Christians are not only victims of Shari'a. They are also the targets of Islamic terrorists attacks.

- In October of 2001, Muslim terrorists opened fire on Christians attending a church in the city of Bahawalpur, killing sixteen people.[131]
- On March 17 of 2002, three masked men entered the International Protestant Church in Islamabad and threw hand grenades in the middle of the worshippers. Four people were killed, including an American woman and her teenage daughter.[132]
- On August 5, 2002, the Murree Christian School—founded in 1956 by American Protestant missionaries—was attacked by a small group of Muslim terrorists carrying weapons and explosives. When the Jihadists were challenged by security guards, they killed two of them, then went on to kill a retired teacher and four others.[133]

- On September 25 two armed men shot and killed seven Pakistani Christians working for the Adara Aman-o-Insaf (Peace and Justice Institute), a human rights organization operating in Karachi. According to police, the two terrorists entered the building, bound and gagged the Christian victims, then shot them at point-blank range.[134]
- On Christmas Day 2002, two assailants, dressed in burqas, threw a bomb into the middle of a worship service at a small church. during a service. Three little girls were killed, and thirteen others were injured. The following day, police arrested a Muslim cleric who had been urging his followers to kill Christians.[135]

International Christian Concern has published seven pages of attacks on Christians, some of them through the legal system, many of them fatal. Yet we hear little about these atrocities, since Pakistan is officially regarded as a friendly Islamic nation.

In today's world, it is again dangerous to be a Christian. The phrase "Christian martyr," which has been consigned to the shelf for generations, now has a new updated meaning. Muslims are ordering Christians to renounce their faith or die. Others aren't even given the choice. They have been murdered, burned out of homes, driven from their country, starved, and even sold into slavery. And these plagues have been visited on them solely because they were Christians.

Why isn't the world up in arms? Certainly you would expect the United States—driven by the outrage of mainstream churches—to rush to the defense of these victims of brutal religious persecution. However, the world, the U.S. government, and even America's churches have been surprisingly unresponsive. Part of their relative disinterest may be the result of an anti-Christian media bias. It is difficult to feel outrage over atrocities you never hear about.

In addition, the U.S. Government, for its own reasons, doesn't want to encourage hostility toward Islamic countries, even when they are guilty of savage religious persecution. "Human rights" is a slippery phrase too often conditioned by politics and economics. If Christians were sitting on half the world's oil supply, the U.S. State Department might be more sympathetic to their plight at the hands of Muslims.

Meanwhile, the killing of Christians continues—and, more often than not, in the name of Allah.

Conclusion

A review of statements and actions by militants in other Islamic nations would reveal the same religious fervor, the same commitment to Jihad. While the majority of Muslims worldwide may well be peace-loving and tolerant of Christians and Jews, it should be obvious that the active minority is a more formidable force in the world today than the passive majority.

The militants, many financially wealthy Saudis and others, are the ones we confront in the international arena and not the peace-loving folks who live next door and worship at the mosque around the corner. The militants are the ones who killed three thousand people—including women and children—on American soil. They are the ones who have declared Jihad on the Jews, the Christians, and the West.

Recognizing the virtues of the majority of Muslims worldwide, we must still decide what to do with Usama bin Laden, the Laskar

Jihad, and the other terrorists who slaughter the innocent in the name of the Prophet.

It simply won't do to say that they are no more than a ragtag gang of isolated fanatics. They control nations with millions of inhabitants—Muslims living under Shari'a as unquestioningly as Americans live under the U.S. Constitution. Such peoples are allowed no information about other religions, no access to or other world views. They are as propaganda-bound as were the citizens of the Soviet Union or the Third Reich. And they cannot be dismissed as irrelevant and un-Muslim.

Nor can the Prophet's words and deeds be airbrushed to pass the muster of political correctness. He was a figure of extravagant virtues, but—from the standpoint of the Judeo-Christian West—he was also a flawed man. PBS and other apologists can talk all they want about Muhammad's gentle spirit and his love of cats, but we must also see him as a vengeful executioner. Too many of his followers have chosen to emulate the darker aspects of his character. A careful examination of the statements and actions of militant Muslims in today's world brings us to three conclusions—one obvious, the other two less apparent.

1. *Militant Islam is engaged in a holy war whose short-term goal is to kill as many Jews and Christians as possible and establish an Islamic hegemony in the Middle East, and whose long-term goal is to conquer the world.*
As extravagant as this goal may seem, it is embraced and voiced by sheikh after sheikh, mullah after mullah. Even while moderate Muslims are protesting that bin Laden and the Ayatollahs misrepresent and debase Islam, the militants are quoting the Qur'an as often and as accurately as their more respectable brethren, illustrating their vision of the Messenger's message with chapter and verse.

The official designation of this struggle as "the War on Terror" is an attempt to render the enemy vague and impersonal—an abstraction rather than flesh-and-blood zealots who are attacking our ships and barracks, crashing airplanes into our buildings, and blowing themselves up in the hope of killing ten of us. Our true adversaries are the mother who cries with joy when she hears her son has committed suicide, the Iranian religious police who inject radioactive materials into Christian prisoners, the African head of state who systematically starves Christians to death in southern Sudan.

To commit these acts in the contemporary world, the enemy must be fighting for more than Jerusalem or a Palestinian homeland. The militant Muslims have told us precisely what they see as their goal. They fight for worldwide triumph of the rule of Islam. With such a prize in mind—and with the promise that martyrs will immediately be taken up to heaven—what can they lose? The sooner we understand this attitude, the more likely we are to survive.

2. *Given the fact that militant Muslims are fighting for Allah, the struggle is unlikely to be resolved by diplomacy, economic measures, or even high-tech military operations.*

In general, the West—grown fat on technology and entrepreneurialism—no longer believes that religion is relevant to domestic affairs, much less to foreign policy. In the United States, leaders of both political parties stress separation of church and state. None would presume to pursue a "Christian diplomacy" abroad. No one in the Department of State could even define what such a phrase might mean.

For this reason, we are ill-equipped to understand and confront an enemy motivated almost solely by religious zealotry. We would like to think that beneath the rhetoric and suicide bombings and cries of Jihad! Jihad! Muslims, like all the rest of us, are really motivated by money. (Former Secretary of State James Baker spoke for the West when he said the conflict was about jobs!)

But suppose that, for Muslims, the struggle really isn't about jobs at all, but about God? Suppose Usama bin Laden really believes that he has been commanded by the Prophet himself to expel the polytheists from the Arabian peninsula? Would this change our strategy?

Maybe, but in order to make such a change, we would have to shed our secularist preconceptions and that change in perspective may be impossible.

The militant Muslim has a mind as sharply focused as a Saracen warrior's. It gives him an enormous advantage over his more secular enemy, and allows him to do things in the name of Allah that civilized Westerners could never contemplate. So this conflict is unique in the experience of Americans—and until we readjust our thinking, we will continue to be vulnerable to terrorist attacks.

3. *Usama bin Laden and other Muslim terrorists count on the United States to be more restrained and more merciful than they are.* Our Judeo-Christian principles are their secret weapon. Bin Laden and other terrorist leaders are well aware that the United States could destroy Mecca, Medina, and all the Arabian oil fields in a matter of hours with well-planned, well-executed nuclear attacks.

So why would they run such a risk by attacking the World Trade Center and the Pentagon?

Because they believe that no risk is involved.

The West no longer believes in holy wars. It believes in peace and the sanctity of human life. The United States bombed

Hiroshima and Nagasaki to prevent greater loss of life, not because Harry Truman believed Christianity was superior to Shintoism. The West, even in its current secular phase, is incapable of killing millions of people and destroying great religious shrines like Medina and Mecca just to wipe out an alien culture. We don't want to harm Islam; we want all faiths and cultures to be able to live together in peace and freedom.

This attitude springs from our Judeo-Christian origins. We may realize that radical Islam is violent and dangerous, but we still hold out hope that they hate us only because they misunderstand us.

The militant Muslims know this. They are counting on America's predominantly Christian sensibilities to restrain us, while they act recklessly, extravagantly in accordance with their own beliefs. They believe they can destroy us because we don't have the faith or courage to destroy them. They see the basic tenets of Christianity, as well as the corruption of our popular culture, as their chief allies in this great Jihad.

How the West behaves in the face of such an enemy is the responsibility of its leaders. However, in order to respond adequately, they must first be willing to understand the ideological (theological) character and dimensions of the threat we face. The American people need to see the face of the enemy, rather imagining a few guerrilla bands or focusing on a meaningless abstraction like Terror.

This book is an attempt to define in their own words and actions the people who are attempting to destroy Israel, America, Judaism, and Christianity. Thus far, the damage they have inflicted is limited, however painful. But remember: There are millions of them and they have their eyes fixed on our nation, our culture, our religious heritage. And if they had the nuclear capability to blow up our part of the world, wiping Jews and Christians from the face of the earth, they would do it without hesitation.

That much is certain.

How You Can Warn America About the Threat of Militant Islam

This small paperback can have a powerful impact on our Country's future safety—if you and others act today.

Please consider giving copies to your friends at home and across America—so **all** Americans can know the truth about militant Islam.

By helping the TVC distribute as many copies as possible—to your local media, to your social and political clubs, and to your church—you can help end the media blackout of this deadly threat to our country. *Please act today!*

Special Bulk Copy Discount Schedule

1 book	$ 4.50	25 books	$35.00	500 books	$375.00
5 books	$12.00	50 books	$65.00	1000 books	$600.00
10 books	$20.00	100 books	$95.00		

All prices include postage and handling.

-- ✂ -----------

T.V.C. Books
P.O. Box 738
Ottawa, IL 61350

**ORDER
TOLL FREE
800-426-1357**

Please send me _____ copies of the paperback edition of *Islam vs. America.* Enclosed is my check for $ _____ or please charge my ☐ Mastercard ☐ Visa

No._____Exp.Date_____

Signature_____

Name_____

Address_____

City_____St._____Zip_____

Illinois residents please add 6.5% sales tax. Please allow 2 weeks for delivery.

How You Can Warn America About the Threat of Militant Islam

This small paperback can have a powerful impact on our Country's future safety—if you and others act today.

Please consider giving copies to your friends at home and across America—so **all** Americans can know the truth about militant Islam.

By helping the TVC distribute as many copies as possible—to your local media, to your social and political clubs, and to your church— you can help end the media blackout of this deadly threat to our country. *Please act today!*

Special Bulk Copy Discount Schedule

1 book $ 4.50	25 books $35.00	500 books $375.00
5 books $12.00	50 books $65.00	1000 books $600.00
10 books $20.00	100 books $95.00	

All prices include postage and handling.

Help Distribute This Book *Free* to 10,000,000 Americans
Contribution Form

Yes, I want to do what I can to help make sure America understands why radical Islam is such a grave threat to freedom, to our civilization and to our very survival.

I agree that Americans aren't hearing the truth about radical Islam from the media, or even from our own government.

Thank you for launching this enormous public education campaign to distribute copies of *Radical Islam vs. America free* to 10,000,000 Americans over the next 90 days ... because we can't effectively protect our civilization from this threat unless Americans understand the religious beliefs that motivate millions of Islamic militants to want to destroy us.

To help you with this enormous effort, *I am sending a donation to* Traditional Values Coalition in the amount of:

☐ $15   (to help distribute 15 books)

☐ $20   (to help distribute 20 books)

☐ $50   (to help distribute 50 books)

☐ $100   (to help distribute 100 books)

☐ Other Donation $_____ (to help distribute as many books as possible)

Name_____

Address_____

City_____ St._____ Zip_____

Phone_____E-mail_____

Please mail your generous donation check to:

Traditional Values Coalition
P.O. Box 5020
Hagerstown, MD 21741-9821

Help Distribute This Book *Free* to 10,000,000 Americans
Contribution Form

Yes, I want to do what I can to help make sure America understands why radical Islam is such a grave threat to freedom, to our civilization and to our very survival.

I agree that Americans aren't hearing the truth about radical Islam from the media, or even from our own government.

Thank you for launching this enormous public education campaign to distribute copies of *Radical Islam vs. America free* to 10,000,000 Americans over the next 90 days … because we can't effectively protect our civilization from this threat unless Americans understand the religious beliefs that motivate millions of Islamic militants to want to destroy us.

To help you with this enormous effort, *I am sending a donation to* Traditional Values Coalition in the amount of:

☐ **$15** (to help distribute 15 books)

☐ **$20** (to help distribute 20 books)

☐ **$50** (to help distribute 50 books)

☐ **$100** (to help distribute 100 books)

☐ Other Donation $_____ (to help distribute as many books as possible)

Name_____

Address_____

City_____St._____Zip_____

Phone_____E-mail_____

Please mail your generous donation check to:

Traditional Values Coalition
P.O. Box 5020
Hagerstown, MD 21741-9821